SRA Imagine It!

Reteach
Annotated Teacher's Edition

Level 4

McGraw Hill **SRA**

Columbus, OH

SRAonline.com

 SRA

Send all inquiries to this address:
SRA/McGraw-Hill
4400 Easton Commons
Columbus, OH 43219-6188

ISBN: 978-0-07-610391-1
MHID: 0-07-610391-9

3 4 5 6 7 8 9 BCH 13 12 11 10 09 08

The **McGraw·Hill** Companies

Unit 1 Risks and Consequences

Unit 2 Nature's Delicate Balance

Unit 3 A Changing America

Unit 4 Science Fair

Unit 5 America on the Move

Unit 6 Dollars and Sense

Name _____   Date _____

Suffixes *-ly* and *-ness*

Focus

A **suffix** is an addition to the end of a word. (ask*ing*)

A **root word** is a word to which a suffix can be added. (*ask*ing)

Adding the suffix **-ly** to the end of words creates adverbs, which describe the way something occurs. (*quickly*)

If the word ends in *y*, the *y* is changed to *i* before adding *-ly*. (*lucky, luckily*)

The suffix **-ness** means "state of." Adding *-ness* to the word *happy* makes the word *happiness*, or the state of being happy.

If the word ends in *y*, the *y* is changed to *i* before adding *-ness*. (*silly, silliness*)

Practice   **Complete the math sentences.**

1. merry – *y* + *i*   +   *-ly*   =   merrily

2. crafty – *y* + *i*   +   *-ness*   =   craftiness

3. hopeless   +   *-ness*   =   hopelessness

4. happy – *y* + *i*   +   *-ly*   =   happily

5. blind   +   *-ness*   =   blindness

6. shabby – *y* + *i*   +   *-ly*   =   shabbily

7. clumsy – *y* + *i*   +   *-ly*   =   clumsily

Name _____   Date _____

Selection Vocabulary

Focus

pursued *v.* past tense of **pursue:** to chase

tides *n.* plural of the noun **tide:** the rise and fall of the sea

lacking *v.* form of **lack:** to be without

fiber *n.* a piece of cloth

cover *v.* to travel over

deserted *adj.* having no people

idly *adv.* not doing anything

dozed *v.* past tense of **doze:** to sleep lightly

Practice   **Fill in each blank with a vocabulary word from this lesson to complete each sentence.**

1. The run-down cabin looked like it might be ____deserted____.

2. The ____tides____ have washed up thousands of seashells on the shore.

3. Mom asked me if I planned on lying around ____idly____ all day.

4. Jenna ____dozed____ off and then woke up with a start.

5. We have a lot of ground to ____cover____ before we stop hiking for the day.

6. The child squealed as she was being ____pursued____ by her sister around the yard.

7. Jack could not make macaroni and cheese because he was ____lacking____ milk.

8. The small square of ____fiber____ was not large enough to use as a blanket.

Name _____ Date _____

Author's Point of View

Focus

Every story is told from a specific point of view that the author chooses. **Point of view** may be first-person or third-person.

In writing a story, the author creates a narrator who tells the story from a particular point of view.

- In a story told from the **first-person point of view,** the narrator is a character in the story. The narrator uses pronouns such as *I, me,* and *my* when telling the story.

- In a story told from the **third-person point of view,** the narrator is an outside observer looking at the happenings in the story. This narrator uses pronouns such as *he, she,* and *they* when telling the story.

Practice A

Look at the sentences below. In the spaces provided, write the point of view of each sentence. Remember, first-person point of view uses pronouns such as *I, me,* and *my.* Third-person point of view uses pronouns such as *he, she,* and *they.*

1. I ride my bicycle to school. _____first-person_____

2. He is afraid of horses. _____third-person_____

3. They enjoyed the movie. _____third-person_____

4. Trevor gave the doll to me. _____first-person_____

5. She practices the piano every day. _____third-person_____

6. My mother baked cookies yesterday. _____first-person_____

Name _____ Date _____

Author's Point of View (continued)

Fill in the sentences below, using pronouns that show the first-person point of view. Use the pronouns *I, me,* and *my.*

7. These are the books that _____ I _____ like.

8. _____ My _____ father delivers mail in the neighborhood.

9. _____ My _____ baby sister looks like Grandma.

10. That belongs to _____ me _____ .

Fill in the sentences below, using pronouns that show the third-person point of view. Use the pronouns *he, she,* and *they.*

11. _____ She or He _____ plays golf every Sunday afternoon.

12. _____ They _____ usually go to the museum together.

13. _____ She _____ is the mother of three children.

14. _____ He or She _____ is an architect.

Practice B **Read the passage below. Then, answer the questions.**

Jerry's grandfather raises cattle on his farm. Jerry helps his grandfather take care of the animals and the crops. They sometimes see deer in the fields, and they enjoy the songs of the many different birds.

What is the point of view of the passage? __ third-person __

Write the word that tells you the point of view. ___ they ___

Name _____ Date _____

Suffixes

Focus
- Remember the **suffixes -ous** and **-ful** mean *full of*
- Remember the **suffix -ly** means *in a certain way*
- Remember the **suffix -ment** means *the result of an action*
- Remember the **suffix -less** means *without*

| joyous | lonely | useful | dangerous | treatment |
| hopeful | movement | careless | hazardous | statement |

Practice

Meaning Strategy
Complete the sentences with spelling words.

1. The wedding reception was a ____joyous____ occasion where the best man
   made a moving ____statement____ about the new bride and groom.

2. Drivers were warned of ____dangerous____ road conditions by the road signs
   that told of ____hazardous____ conditions ahead.

3. The ____lonely____ kitten meowed and made a quick, playful ____movement____
   toward its owner.

4. After he realized he forgot to lock the door, he was ____hopeful____ that his
   ____careless____ action would not cause any problems.

5. After getting ____treatment____ for a cold, the student returned to school
   feeling like she could be a more ____useful____ participant in class.

Name _____   Date _____

Concrete Nouns and Abstract Nouns

 Focus
Nouns are words that name persons, places, things, or ideas.

A **concrete noun** names something we can touch or see. *(house, boy)*

An **abstract noun** names something we cannot touch or see, such as an idea or emotion. *(fun, sadness)*

 **Practice**
Decide whether the following nouns are concrete or abstract. Circle the correct word.

1. **kite** (concrete/abstract)

2. **jealousy** (concrete/abstract)

3. **fear** (concrete/abstract)

4. **movie** (concrete/abstract)

5. **friendship** (concrete/abstract)

 **Apply**
Write a sentence using each of these abstract nouns.

6. **anger** ___**Possible Answer** He stormed through the door full of anger.___

7. **decision** ___**Possible Answer** I have a big decision to make before tomorrow.___

Name _____ Date _____

Prefixes *re-*, *un-*, and *en-*

Focus

A **prefix** is an addition to the beginning of a word. (*un*true)

A **root word** is a word to which a prefix can be added. (un*true*)

The prefix **re-** means "again." To *re*view is to view again.

The prefix **un-** means "not." If something is *un*fair, it is not fair.

The prefix **en-** means "to make a certain way." *En*rich means to make rich.

Use these words to complete the exercise below.

unplanned	unfit	redress	enthrone
unbeaten	review	redirect	entrap

Practice Add the prefix *re-, un-,* or *en-* to each root word to make a new word.

1. throne ___enthrone___

2. dress ___redress___

3. fit ___unfit___

4. beaten ___unbeaten___

5. direct ___redirect___

6. planned ___unplanned___

7. view ___review___

8. trap ___entrap___

Name _____ Date _____

Selection Vocabulary

Focus

hastened hurried *v.* past tense of **hasten:** to hurry

shuddered shook *v.* past tense of **shudder:** to shake with horror

despairing *adj.* without hope

sympathetic *adj.* understanding; having a kind feeling for someone

delivered saved *v.* past tense of **deliver:** to save from danger

flickering *adj.* becoming brighter and then darker over and over

companion *n.* a person who is traveling with someone else

concealed hidden *v.* past tense of **conceal:** to hide

Practice **Write the vocabulary word next to the group of words that have a similar meaning.**

1. rescued; freed; saved ___delivered___

2. flashing; twinkling; brightening ___flickering___

3. compassionate; understanding; gentle ___sympathetic___

4. partner; friend; buddy ___companion___

5. hopeless; discouraged; depressed ___despairing___

6. covered; hidden; disguised ___concealed___

7. hurried; rushed; sped ___hastened___

8. shivered; shook; trembled ___shuddered___

Name _____ Date _____

Prefixes

Focus
- Remember, the **prefix re-** means *again.*
- Remember, the **prefixes dis-** and **un-** mean the *opposite of.*
- Remember, the **prefix mid-** means *in the middle of.*

disagree	disappear	discount	midterm	review
uncover	rewind	midnight	displace	undone

Practice

Visualization Strategy
Rewrite the word correctly.

1. dissagree _____disagree_____

2. disapear _____disappear_____

3. diskount _____discount_____

4. midturm _____midterm_____

5. reveiw _____review_____

6. uncuver _____uncover_____

7. rewinde _____rewind_____

8. midnite _____midnight_____

9. displce _____displace_____

10. undun _____undone_____

Name _____ Date _____

Action Verbs

 **Focus**
An **action verb** shows what the subject does. The action can be seen or unseen.

Example: Molly **thought** about her idea.

 **Practice**
Circle the action verb in each sentence. On the line, write a different action verb that would also fit in the sentence. The first one is done for you.

1. Jayme (went) to the store. **Possible Answer** drove _____

2. I (dropped) the ball. **Possible Answer** caught _____

3. Gavin (loves) trucks. **Possible Answer** dislikes _____

4. I (failed) the test. **Possible Answer** took _____

5. Felisa (ate) lunch. **Possible Answer** skipped _____

6. Link (handed) the baby a toy. **Possible Answer** gave _____

Name _____ Date _____

Suffixes -y, -ful, and -less

Focus

The suffix **-y** means "being," "having."

Examples: rain*y* = having rain; funn*y* = being fun.

The suffix **-ful** means "full of." Example: cheer*ful* = full of cheer.

The suffix **-less** means "without." Example: pain*less* = without pain.

Note: When adding -y to a word, if the word has one syllable and ends with a short vowel and consonant, double the final consonant before adding -y.

Example: (*fun, funny*)

Practice Circle the word that makes sense in the sentence.

1. I was happy that my trip to the dentist was (painful, (painless)).

2. Ingrid got completely soaked on this ((rainy) rainless) day.

3. I would be terribly sad if I found myself (friendful, (friendless)) at the party.

4. If Fran is ((careless), careful) while crossing the street, she could get hurt.

5. Marie is in a ((grouchy), grouchless) mood for some reason.

6. The food was so ((spicy), spiceless) I drank a whole glass of water.

7. Most babies are born (toothy, (toothless)).

Name _____   Date _____

Selection Vocabulary

Focus

merriment *n.* fun

tangled wrapped *v.* past tense of **tangle:** to wrap in a mess of strings

miserable *adj.* very unhappy

obviously *adv.* in a way that is easy to see

recalled remembered *v.* past tense of **recall:** to remember

gnawing chewing *v.* form of **gnaw:** to chew

cover *n.* something that would be good to hide behind

circumstances *n.* plural of **curcumstance:** the way things are at the moment

Practice   **Circle the word in parentheses that best fits each sentence.**

1. My dog Bilbo is always (tangled/gnawing) on a bone.

2. Given the (circumstances/cover), she is lucky to be alive.

3. As the rain pelted down, the two boys ran for (miserable/cover).

4. Riley laughed and joined in the (merriment/miserable).

5. I tried not to get (recalled/tangled) up in the rope, but it was no use.

6. Shanna (recalled/obviously) the day she lost her first tooth.

7. You can tell by the dark clouds that a storm is (gnawing/obviously) on the way.

8. My aching tooth is making me (circumstances/miserable).

Name _____ Date _____

Cause and Effect

Focus Cause and effect relationships help readers understand why events happen in a certain way.

- A **cause** is why something happens.
- The **effect** is what happens as a result.

Cause	Effect
The boy kicked the ball $\longrightarrow$	The ball flew through the air.

Writers sometimes use signal words to show cause and effect relationships. Signal words, such as *because, so, if, then,* and *since,* help the reader know what happens and why it happens.

Practice A Match each cause with its effect by drawing a line.

Cause

1. Cake batter is poured into a pan and placed into a hot oven.

2. An apple seed is planted.

3. Ice cubes and water are added to instant tea.

4. The bird flaps its wings.

5. A light switch on a wall is flipped up to the "on" position.

Effect

a. An apple tree grows.

b. Iced tea is made.

c. A light is turned on.

d. A cake bakes.

e. The bird flies.

Name _____   Date _____

Practice B

Look at the following sentences. Some of the sentences show a cause and effect relationship. Others do not. Draw an *X* next to the sentences that show a cause and effect relationship. Look for signal words such as *since*, *if*, *so*, *then*, or *because*. Underline the signal words in the sentences that show cause and effect.

6. __X__ <u>Because</u> Jason threw a baseball at a front window of the house, the window broke.

7. _____ The cow jumped over the moon and bumped into a star.

8. _____ Spencer rode his bike to school and then to the library.

9. __X__ <u>Since</u> the lock was broken, the Johnsons no longer store their tools in the shed.

10. __X__ <u>If</u> the cookies are gone, <u>then</u> someone must have eaten them.

11. _____ The jacket belongs to Karen, who forgot it at the game.

12. __X__ The dog's house is empty, <u>so</u> she must be elsewhere.

13. __X__ I hear a bell ringing, <u>so</u> it must be the telephone.

14. _____ The computer is new, and is sitting on the student's desk.

15. __X__ <u>Because</u> it is raining, I will wear a raincoat.

16. _____ The cat usually attacked small animals.

Apply

Write an effect for the following cause.

Because it is warm outdoors, _____

Name _____ **Date** _____

Spelling Changes with Affixes

Focus The spelling of base words may change when affixes are added.

- Words ending in a silent *e* usually drop the *e* before adding the suffix that begins with a vowel.

- The base word *solve* plus the affix *-able* is formed when the silent *e* is dropped and *-able* is added to create *solvable*. Drop the silent *e* at the end of base words when adding a suffix that begins with a vowel.

- For base words that end in *y* and are preceded by a consonant, change the *y* to an *i* when adding a suffix that begins with a vowel.

| angrily | pollution | envious | flammable | erosion |
| basically | courteous | memorable | solvable | usable |

Practice **Meaning Strategy**
Add an affix to each base to form a spelling word.

1. angry _____angrily_____

2. pollute _____pollution_____

3. envy _____envious_____

4. flame _____flammable_____

5. erode _____erosion_____

6. basic _____basically_____

7. courtesy _____courteous_____

8. memory _____memorable_____

9. solve _____solvable_____

10. use _____usable_____

Name _____ Date _____

Linking Verbs

Focus

A **linking verb** does not show action. Linking verbs connect the subject of a sentence with a noun or adjective that renames or describes the subject.

Example: David **is** a good friend.

In the sentence above, the linking verb = **is**. It links the words *David* and *friend.*

Practice

If the underlined word is a linking verb, write *yes*. If it is not a linking verb, write *no*. Remember, a linking verb connects the subject with a word that describes it.

1. I <u>will</u> read the book tonight. ___no___

2. Kami and Aly <u>are</u> nice girls. ___yes___

3. Our new car <u>is</u> red. ___yes___

4. Carly <u>is</u> looking for her bag. ___no___

5. Your dog <u>looks</u> well-groomed. ___yes___

6. The bus driver <u>was</u> late. ___yes___

7. I <u>should</u> exercise after school. ___no___

8. Animals <u>are</u> fascinating to study. ___yes___

Name _____ **Date** _____

Words Ending in *-s, -es, -ed,* and *-ing*

Focus

When making singular nouns plural, remember:

Add *-es* to words that end in *sh, ch, ss, s,* and *x* to form plurals.

In words that end with consonant + *-y,* the *y* is changed to *i* before **-es** is added.

Also remember:

Verbs that end in **-ed** are past tense.

Verbs ending in **-ing** are present tense.

Practice **Circle the correct verb in parentheses.**

1. She (jumped, jumping) down from the platform and landed on both feet.

2. Why is that little boy (smiled, smiling) at you?

3. He (crashed, crashing) his toy car into the wall.

4. William (decided, deciding) not to try out for soccer this year.

5. Kohl is (cheered, cheering) loudly for his little sister.

Circle the words that are spelled correctly.

6. bikeing   biking

7. joging   jogging

8. clapped   claped

9. exploreing   exploring

10. leaped   leapped

Name _____ Date _____

Selection Vocabulary

Focus

tensely *adv.* feeling emotional strain

pleading begging *v.* form of **plead:** to beg

paces walks *v.* present tense of **pace:** to walk back and forth

opportunities chances *n.* plural of **opportunity:** a chance to succeed in life

decent *adj.* good enough to make someone comfortable

stable *adj.* steady; dependable

concerned *adj.* showing worry

strive *v.* to work to get something

Practice   Match each word on the left to its definition on the right.

1. stable

2. decent

3. paces

4. strive

5. opportunities

6. concerned

7. tensely

8. pleading

a. begging

b. chances to succeed in life

c. good enough to make someone comfortable

d. feeling emotional strain

e. walks back and forth

f. showing worry

g. work to get something

h. steady, dependable

Name _____ Date _____

Author's Purpose

Focus

Writers have reasons for writing a story in a certain way. The **author's purpose** is the reason a story is written a certain way. An author's purpose

- can be to *inform,* to *explain,* to *entertain,* or to *persuade.*
- affects things in the story such as the *details, description, story events,* and *dialogue.*

An author can have more than one purpose for writing a story.

Practice A

Look at the following sentences. Write an X next to each sentence that informs the reader. Sentences that inform contain facts and information.

1. __X__ The car is one of the primary forms of transportation in the United States.

2. _____ The queen, her family, and the entire kingdom lived happily ever after.

3. __X__ The cocker spaniel is a type of dog.

4. __X__ Mark Twain is the author of many novels and essays.

Look at the following sentences. Write an X next to each sentence that explains something. Writing that explains something may describe how something works.

5. __X__ To open the door, you must lift the lever and push.

6. _____ Most children like orange juice.

Name _____ Date _____

Author's Purpose

Practice B **Look at the following sentences. Write an _X_ next to each sentence that entertains the reader.**
Writing that entertains the reader has story events, dialogue, or details that are sometimes humorous or funny.

7. _____ We own two horses and three cows.

8. __X__ The silly dog laughed until the cows came home.

9. __X__ Mickey and the talking frog became good friends.

10. __X__ The teacup asked the dish what he thought about Mr. Tibbs.

11. _____ A dictionary lists words in alphabetical order.

Look at the following sentences. Write an _X_ next to the ones that persuade. Writing that persuades tries to get the reader to think or act a certain way.

12. __X__ You should buy this brand of milk.

13. _____ The boy gave his last cent to charity.

14. _____ The tiger at the zoo looks fierce.

15. _____ They waited in line for hours to buy movie tickets.

16. __X__ You must come to dinner tomorrow evening.

Apply **Write a sentence that informs, explains, entertains, or persuades the reader about the following topics.**

An animal: _____

A book: _____

Name _____ **Date** _____

Inflectional Endings

Focus
- For many base words, simply add the **inflectional endings.**
- Drop silent *e* before adding *-ed* and *-ing*.
- When a word ends in *consonant-y,* change the *y* to *i* and add the ending.
- Double the final consonant before adding the endings *-ed* and *-ing* to words that contain a short vowel sound.

unplugged	curved	stripped	bleached	worried
striped	insisted	rating	controlled	shedding

Practice **Meaning Strategy**
Choose the spelling word that correctly completes the sentence.

1. The (curved, striped) around past the lake.

2. The (striped, stripped) wallpaper gave the room an interesting look.

3. The (controlled, worried) look on her face let them know the situation was serious.

4. She (insisted, worried) that her friend stay for dinner.

Apply Add the ending to the word and write it on the blank. Remember, you may need to change the base word before adding the ending.

5. unplug + ed = _____unplugged_____

6. curve + ed = _____curved_____

7. strip + ed = _____stripped_____

8. bleach + ed = _____bleached_____

9. stripe + ed = _____striped_____

10. rate + ing = _____rating_____

11. control + ed = _____controlled_____

12. shed + ing = _____shedding_____

Name _____ Date _____

Personal Object Pronouns

Focus

A **pronoun** is used in place of one or more nouns.

Like nouns, pronouns can be subjects or objects in a sentence.

A pronoun that receives the action of the verb is the *direct object.* (The dog chased **me.**)

A pronoun at the end of a preposition is the *object of the preposition.* (The kite sailed over **her.**)

Personal pronouns name specific people or things.

Personal object pronouns are *me, you, him, her, it, us, you,* and *them.*

Practice

Circle the personal object pronouns in each sentence. Some sentences have more than one.

1. I don't want to make (him) wait on (me.)

2. Dad said he would take (us) to the baseball game tonight.

3. Ask (him) what his name is.

4. I took (it) off the shelf and dusted (it.)

5. She couldn't tell (me) the answer.

6. Lara wanted to go to the movie with (them.)

7. Did she take your lunch away from (you)?

Name _____ Date _____

Compound Words

Focus A **compound word** is a word that is made of two or more smaller words. *(playmate, timetable)*

Prefixes and suffixes are not compound words. *(un•fair, play•ed)*

Practice Use these words to complete the exercise below.

waterfall	grapevine	sometimes	brainstorm	billboard
earthquake	headache	fireplace	outfit	footprint

Compound Word Strategy
Replace one of the words in each compound word to write a spelling word.

1. somewhere _____ sometimes

2. brainwash _____ brainstorm

3. headstone _____ headache

4. fireman _____ fireplace

5. outdoors _____ outfit

6. waterhole _____ waterfall

7. grapefruit _____ grapevine

8. footpath _____ footprint

9. earthworm _____ earthquake

10. billfold _____ billboard

Name _____ Date _____

Selection Vocabulary

Focus

brilliant *adj.* bright

spread *v.* to open outward

luxurious *adj.* rich and comfortable

plunged *v.* past tense of **plunge:** to fall

nudged *v.* past tense of **nudge:** to push slightly

crowed *v.* past tense of **crow:** to brag loudly

astonishment *n.* a sudden wonder

Practice   **Circle the correct word that completes each sentence.**

1. Those pillows on her bed are _____.
   a. spread   **b.** (luxurious)   **c.** nudged

2. He _____ his arms and wrapped his son in a bear hug.
   a. nudged   **b.** crowed   **c.** (spread)

3. She _____ with pride after he won the race.
   a. (crowed)   **b.** plunged   **c.** spread

4. The light from that huge lantern is quite _____.
   a. (brilliant)   **b.** luxurious   **c.** astonishment

5. Will gasped in sheer _____.
   a. spread   **b.** brilliant   **c.** (astonishment)

6. Norah _____ me so I would stay awake.
   a. plunged   **b.** (nudged)   **c.** crowed

7. Maylin _____ into the pool by accident.
   a. (plunged)   **b.** spread   **c.** nudged

Name _____ Date _____

Compound Words

Compound words are formed by joining together two words. Some words that make up compounds words may have one or more syllables.

Sometimes compound words combine the meanings of the two smaller words they contain.

highway	**coastline**	**flashlight**	**whenever**	**basketball**
nowhere	**sometimes**	**eyesight**	**handlebar**	**worldwide**

 **Proofreading Strategy** Circle the misspelled words and write them correctly.

1. The (hiway) followed the (costeline). _____highway_____ _____coastline_____

2. (Somtimes) I play soccer with my sister. _____sometimes_____

3. I used a (flashlite) when my (eyesite) became weak. _____flashlight_____
_____eyesight_____

4. (Wenever) I read about a (werldwid) epidemic, I get nervous. _____whenever_____
_____worldwide_____

5. I looked for my (basckatball), but it was (nowear) to be found. _____basketball_____
_____nowhere_____

6. My (handelbarr) was loose after the crash. _____handlebar_____

Name _____ Date _____

Complete Subjects and Predicates

Focus

The **simple subject** of a sentence is a *noun* that tells *whom* or *what* the sentence is about.

The **simple predicate** of a sentence is a *verb* that tells what the subject *does.*

The **complete subject** includes all the words that describe the subject.

The **complete predicate** includes all the words that follow the predicate.

Example: The brilliantly-colored lorikeet landed on her shoulder.

Simple subject = lorikeet

Simple predicate = landed

Complete subject = The brilliantly-colored lorikeet

Complete predicate = landed on her shoulder

Practice   **In each of the following sentences, circle the simple subject, and underline the simple predicate.**

1. Kate's (father) cleaned the garage.

2. Kate's (father) cleaned the garage yesterday for six hours.

3. Our whole (class) rode the bus to the museum.

4. The (water) from the river overflowed into our yard.

5. The chubby little (chipmunk) stuffed its cheeks with seeds.

6. Sarah's (grandmother) baked us a batch of delicious cookies.

Name _____   **Date** _____

Greek Roots

> **Focus** English words also contain parts, or roots, that have been borrowed from the ancient language of Greek. When you know the meaning of a **Greek root,** you can begin to figure out the meaning of the English word that contains it. Here are some common Greek roots and affixes and their meanings. The affixes are circled.
>
> **micro** = small   **tele** = far off   (**graph** = to write)   **therm** = heat
> **gram** = to write   **log** = word   (**logy** = the study of)   **phon** = sounds
>
> The word *telephone* has the Greek roots **tele** and **phon,** which mean "far off" and "sounds." You can tell from the meaning of the Greek roots that a telephone is a device that allows you to hear sounds from far off or far away.

Practice   **Circle the Greek root in the following words. Then, write the meaning of the Greek root next to the word.**

1. dia(log)ue   log means word

2. (micro)scope   micro means small

3. (tele)vision   tele means far off

4. (phono)graph   phono means sound

5. (therm)ostat   therm means heat

Name _____ Date _____

Selection Vocabulary

Focus

jagged *adj.* having sharp points that stick out

trickled *v.* past tense of **trickle:** to run slowly in a series of drops or a thin stream

flowed *v.* past tense of **flow:** to move as water does

raging *adj.* violent, wild

irrigation *adj.* having to do with supplying farmland with water

reservoir *n.* a lake for storing water

particles *n.* tiny pieces

glacier *n.* a huge mass of ice formed from unmelted snow, usually found in the polar regions or in high mountains

Practice Circle the word in parentheses that best fits each sentence.

1. The last drops of water (particles/(trickled)) out of the hose.

2. I would hate to get caught in a ((raging)/trickled) hurricane.

3. Jerry's farm needs a complicated ((irrigation)/flowed) system because it is so large.

4. There are little (reservoir/(particles)) of cereal floating in the milk.

5. Have you been to the (glacier/(reservoir)) right outside the city?

6. I hope their ship doesn't hit a (reservoir/(glacier)) in the icy water.

7. The river ((flowed)/trickled) quickly down the steep mountain.

8. Be careful climbing those (raging/(jagged)) rocks!

Name _____ Date _____

Sequence

Focus **Sequence** is the order in which things happen in a story. A writer uses time and order words to help the reader follow the sequence in a story.

- **Order words** show the order in which things take place. Words such as *first, then, next,* and *finally* show order.

- **Time words** show how time passes in a story. Words such as *spring, tomorrow,* and *morning* show time.

Practice A Look at the pictures. Put the pictures in the proper sequence. Write the correct order word in the space below each picture. Use the order words *first, then,* and *finally.*

then

first

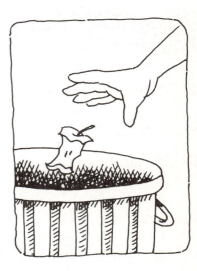

finally

Name _____ **Date** _____

Sequence

Practice B Look at the following sentences about "The Snowflake: A Water Cycle Story." Put the sentences in the proper sequence. Write the correct order word in front of the sentence. Use the order words *first, next,* and *finally.*

1. _____ next _____ The snowflake floats slowly downward with thousands of other flakes.

2. _____ finally _____ The snowflake comes to rest on the jagged peak of a mountain.

3. _____ first _____ The snowflake falls from a great gray cloud.

Look at the following sentences. Complete each sentence by filling in a time word. Use the time words in the box below. **Answers will vary.**

soon summer	winter yesterday	afternoon morning

4. I will eat breakfast in the __**Possible Answer** morning__.

5. Ken walked to the park __**Possible Answer** yesterday__.

6. Lunch is usually served in the __**Possible Answer** afternoon__.

7. __**Possible Answer** Soon__ it will be Christmas.

8. The big snowstorm in New York happened last __**Possible Answer** winter__.

9. During the __**Possible Answer** summer__, it gets very hot in Texas.

10. We will visit Uncle Bob __**Possible Answer** soon__.

Comprehension Skill • *Reteach*

Name _____ Date _____

Greek Roots

Focus

The Greek root **phon** means "sound."

- The Greek root **demos** means "people."
- The Greek root **path** means "feeling."
- The Greek root **derm** means "skin."
- The Greek root **historia** means "learning" or "knowing."
- The Greek root **kardia** (or **cardia**) means "heart."

pathetic	cardiology	empathy	cardiac	microphone
historian	pandemic	demography	dermatology	pathetic

Practice

Meaning Strategy
Complete the sentences with spelling words.

1. The museum hired an ____*historian*____ to teach a class on the Civil War.

2. The speaker used a ____*microphone*____ so that everyone could hear.

3. She decided to study ____*dermatology*____ in medical school.

4. He made a ____*pathetic*____ attempt to do his homework at the last minute.

5. Because he was fascinated by the heart, Steven decided to study ____*cardiology*____.

Apply

Fill in the missing letters and write the spelling word on the blank.

6. ca_rd_i_ _a_c   ____*cardiac*____

7. de_m_o_gra_p_hy   ____*demography*____

8. pan_dem_i_c   ____*pandemic*____

9. emp_a_th_y_   ____*empathy*____

10. p_a_th_et_i_c   ____*pathetic*____

***Reteach* • Spelling**

Name _____ Date _____

What Is a Sentence?

Focus

Rule	Example
• A **sentence** has two parts—a subject and a predicate. The **subject** of a sentence tells who or what the sentence is about.	• **Caleb** called his mother. **Happiness** is an emotion.
• The **predicate** of a sentence tells something about the subject.	• Jose **walked down the street.**

Practice Complete the sentences in the chart below with a subject or predicate from the box.

a salmon run	a time line	is a book of facts	is in Asia

Subject	Predicate
A time line	shows events in the order they happened.
A salmon run	is the yearly return of salmon to lay eggs in freshwater rivers.
An almanac	is a book of facts.
China	is in Asia.

Grammar, Usage, and Mechanics • *Reteach*

Name _____ Date _____

Latin Roots

> **Focus** English words often contain roots from the ancient languages of Greek and Latin. These roots may be found in a variety of words, and have the same meaning no matter where you find them. When you know the meaning of a **Latin root**, you can begin to figure out the meaning of the English word that contains it. Here are some common **Latin roots** and affixes and their meanings:
>
> **trans** = "across"   **cred** = "believe"   **aud** = "hear"   **doc** = "teach"
> **anim** = "life"   **cap** = "head"   **dent** = "tooth"   **vis** = "to see"
>
> The word *dentist* has the Latin root **dent,** which means "tooth." You can tell from the meaning of the Latin root that a dentist is a person who takes care of your teeth.

Practice **Read each sentence and answer the question below it.**

1. The cars were <u>transported</u> from America to Europe by ship.

   What does transported mean? <u>to carry from one place to another; to move</u>

   <u>across.</u>

2. We did not give <u>credit</u> to her story; we thought she was a liar.

   What does credit mean? <u>belief in the truth of something</u>

3. The music is barely <u>audible</u>. I can't hear it and neither can the people outside.

   What does audible mean? <u>loud enough to hear</u>

4. A birth certificate is a <u>document</u> that lists the day you were born.

   What is a document? <u>a printed statement that contains some type of</u>

   <u>information about something.</u>

Name _____ Date _____

Selection Vocabulary

 **Focus**

energy *n.* the power to do work

transferred *v.* past tense of **transfer:** to pass along

soar *v.* to fly high

release *v.* to let loose

fuels *n.* plural form of **fuel:** something that gives out energy as it is burned

contains *v.* present tense of **contain:** to hold

stored *adj.* having been put away for future use

eventually *adv.* sooner or later

 **Practice** **Write T in the blank if the sentence for the vocabulary word is correct. Write F if the sentence is false. For each F answer, write the word that fits the definition.**

1. *Transferred* means "passed along."

   _____T_____   _____

2. If you *store* something, it is let loose.

   _____F_____   _____release_____

3. If you do something *eventually*, you do it sooner or later.

   _____T_____   _____

4. *Energy* means "put away for future use."

   _____F_____   _____Stored_____

5. If a box *fuels* something, it "holds" it.

   _____F_____   _____contains_____

Name _____ Date _____

Main Idea and Details

Focus

The main idea is what a paragraph is about. Details in the paragraph support the main idea.

A paragraph has a main idea and details that support the main idea.

- The **main idea** is the most important point the writer makes. The main idea is often stated in a clear topic sentence. The topic sentence is usually at the beginning or at the end of a paragraph.

- The other sentences in a paragraph have **details**, or information, that describe the main idea more fully.

Practice A

Look at the main ideas and details. Write an _X_ next to the sentence that describes the main idea more fully.

1. Main idea: As a child, Mae dreamed of being a scientist.

___X___ She loved working on science projects in school.

_____ She took dancing lessons.

_____ She helped her mother cook dinner after school.

2. Main idea: Trevor loves animals.

_____ He walks to school every morning.

_____ He loves chocolate ice cream.

___X___ He works with his father at the animal shelter.

Name _____ Date _____

Main Idea and Details

**Practice B** **Read the following paragraph, and answer the questions.**

    Over the years, Girl Scouting has become very popular in the United States. Juliette Gordon Low started the Girl Scouts of the U.S.A. in 1912. When she died in 1927, there were more than 160,000 Girl Scouts in the United States. Today, millions of girls belong to Girl Scout troops across the nation. **Answers will vary.** Possible answers are shown.

3. What is this paragraph about? Write the sentence that contains

the main idea. **Possible Answer** Over the years, Girl Scouting has become

very popular in the United States.

4. Now look for sentences with details that support the main idea. Write one sentence that contains details that describe the main idea

more fully. **Possible Answer** When she died in 1927, there were more than

160,000 Girl Scouts in the United States.

**Apply** **Look at the following paragraph. The main idea is missing. Figure out the main idea from the details in the sentences. Then, write the main idea on the lines below.**

    Vanilla is my mother's favorite flavor. My little sister loves strawberry ice cream. Dad usually gets banana ice cream. My favorite flavor is chocolate.

Possible Answer Everyone in my family has a different favorite flavor of ice

cream.

Name _____ Date _____

Latin Roots

Focus

The Latin root **dict** means "say" or "speak."
- The Latin root **scribe** means "write."
- The Latin roots **port** and **fer** mean "carry."
- The Latin root **creat** means "to make new."

defer	creature	dictate	creative	diction
subscribe	scribble	referral	report	export

Practice

Meaning Strategy
Write a sentence using each of the spelling words.
Sentence will vary

1. _____

2. _____

3. _____

4. _____

5. _____

6. _____

7. _____

8. _____

9. _____

10. _____

Name _____ Date _____

Quotation Marks

Focus

- Use **quotation marks** around the exact words of a speaker.

Example: "Early to bed, early to rise makes a man healthy, wealthy, and wise," said Benjamin Franklin.

- Use **quotation marks** around the title of a poem or short story.

Example: The longest poem ever written is the Indian epic "Mahabharata."

Practice Place quotation marks around the titles of the poems in the following sentences.

1. One of my favorite poems is Lemonade Stand. "Lemonade Stand."

2. My brother wrote a poem called A Day in My Big Life.

   "A Day in My Big Life."

3. The Raven is a well-known poem by Edgar Allan Poe. "The Raven"

Write an answer to each question using a line of dialogue. Be sure to use quotation marks correctly.

4. "Why weren't you in school yesterday?" Aimee asked Mindy.

   Possible Answer "I was sick," Mindy said.

5. "How did you meet your best friend?" Diego's mom asked him.

   Possible Answer "We were both on the same soccer team," Diego said.

Name _____ Date _____

Synonyms

Synonyms are words that have similar meanings.

Examples of Synonyms: **fat** and **plump**
large and **big**
begin and **start**

Use these words to complete the exercise.

certain	painting	fixing	job	commotion

Use the words in the box to write a synonym for each underlined word.

1. My <u>occupation</u> is mailcarrier. ____job_____

2. I enjoy <u>restoring</u> broken things. ___fixing_____

3. There is a <u>mural</u> on the wall of my apartment. ___painting_____

4. I am <u>confident</u> I wrote the correct answer to the question. ___certain_____

5. The dogs running through the crowd at the parade caused a <u>disturbance</u>.

____commotion____

Name _____ Date _____

Selection Vocabulary

Focus

linked *adj.* past tense of **link**: to connect

slightly *adv.* by a little bit

depend *v.* to need, to rely

microscope *n.* a tool for looking at very small things

bitterly *adv.* harshly; extremely

seaweed *n.* a plant that grows near the surface of the sea

branch *v.* to divide and subdivide

Practice   **Write the word that best fits each clue below.**

1. Jason gathered some plants that had washed up from the ocean.

   What were they? _____seaweed_____

2. This piece of scientific equipment is not a telescope but is used to

   see tinier things. What is it? _____microscope_____

3. Food chains divide and subdivide. We might say they do

   what? _____branch_____

4. What word is commonly used to describe how the pieces of a

   chain are hooked together? _____linked_____

5. If the freezing wind and rain hurt your hands and face, you might

   say they have stung you how? _____bitterly_____

6. Natalie can wiggle her tooth just a little bit. We might say she can

   wiggle it how? _____slightly_____

Name _____ **Date** _____

Making Inferences

Making inferences helps a reader understand the total picture in a story.

An **inference** is a statement you make about a character or an event in a story when you read.

Here is what you use to make an inference.

- First, use **information** from the story. Facts and descriptions in a story are types of information you can use to make an inference.

- Combine the information from the story with your **personal experience** or knowledge to make an inference.

Practice A **Read the paragraph below. Then answer the following questions.**

The day that Ted broke his arm started out like most days. He struggled out of bed and ate breakfast. Then he looked at the kitchen clock. He had only three minutes to get to the bus stop! Ted grabbed his bookbag and flew out the door. He wished he had seen the family's dog standing outside the door. He tripped over her and landed on the wooden steps. The rest of the story is too painful to tell!

A fact is information you can use to make an inference. In the paragraph above, one fact is that Ted runs out the door to catch the bus. Write another fact from the passage.

Possible Answer Ted broke his arm.

_____

Make an inference based on the above paragraph.

Possible Answer Ted broke his arm by tripping over the dog.

_____

Name _____ Date _____

Making Inferences

Practice B Read the following paragraphs. Think about the information in each paragraph and your personal knowledge or experience. Then complete each inference below with the correct word.

The sky was gray. It was a cold day that Thursday morning in November. The children were excited. Soon, they would be on their way to their grandmother's house. They could not help but think of the special dinner they would eat, including turkey, mashed potatoes, and stuffing. Grandmother always had the best desserts, too.

Inference: The children are going to their grandmother's

house to celebrate **Possible Answer** Thanksgiving
_____.

"Aha! Here it is!" Ben exclaimed.

He had been looking for his pet's leash for hours. Ben chuckled as he pulled the leash from under the sofa. He also found a rubber bone and an old shoe Snooper loved to chew.

"Snooper is very, very smart," Ben said to himself. Snooper probably hid the leash because he did not want to see Dr. Watson. Snooper hated getting shots and did not care for Dr. Watson.

Inference: Snooper is what type of animal? **Possible Answer** a dog
_____

Apply Make another inference from the passage about Ben and Snooper. Write your statement here.
Answers will vary.
Possible Answer Snooper is an older dog, not a puppy.
_____

_____

Name _____ **Date** _____

Synonyms

Focus | **Synonyms** are words that have similar meanings, but they don't always mean exactly the same thing. Synonyms express shades of meaning.

Examples: *old* and *ancient*

spotted	merry	spied	happy	viewed
cheerful	slightly	collide	somewhat	crash

Practice | **Meaning Strategy**
Write the spelling word(s) that has a similar meaning.

Use the words in the box to write a synonym for each underlined word.

1. noticed   <u>spotted</u>   <u>spied</u>   <u>viewed</u>

2. glad   <u>merry</u>   <u>happy</u>   <u>cheerful</u>

3. sort of   <u>somewhat</u>   <u>slightly</u>

4. smash   <u>crash</u>   <u>collide</u>

Name _____ Date _____

Compound Subjects

Focus A **compound subject** is two or more subjects that have the same predicate in a sentence.

Example: **Brian and Missy** live in San Francisco.

The verb in a sentence must agree in number with the subject in a sentence.

Example: Will likes green salad. Will and Polly like green salad.

Practice **Fill in the blanks with a compound subject of your choice.**

1. **Possible Answer** Kendra and her friend _____ played together all afternoon.

2. **Possible Answer** My mom and dad _____ sing like birds.

3. **Possible Answer** The cows and horses _____ came all the way from Alabama.

Circle the verb in parentheses that agrees in number with the subject in the sentence.

4. Vera and I (jump/jumps) rope whenever we go to her house.

5. My little sister (talk/talks) all the time.

6. Jillian's dad and uncle (build/builds) houses for a living.

7. The soccer season and the football season (begin/begins) at the same time.

8. Fresh strawberries (is/are) my favorite treat.

Name _____ **Date** _____

Antonyms

Antonyms are words that are opposite or almost the opposite of another word.

front and **back**   **left** and **right**

Use these words to complete the exercise below.

young	slender	proper	hot	close
tall	rapid	dark	firm	poor

Complete the antonym pairs with a word from the box.

1. slow _____ rapid _____

2. soft _____ firm _____

3. wrong _____ proper _____

4. old _____ young _____

5. fat _____ slender _____

6. rich _____ poor _____

7. cold _____ hot _____

8. light _____ dark _____

9. short _____ tall _____

10. open _____ close _____

Name _____ Date _____

Selection Vocabulary

Focus

shrivel *v.* to wrinkle and become small (page 194)

droop *v.* to sink; to hang down (page 195)

brittle *adj.* easily broken (page 195)

decays *v.* present tense of **decay:** to slowly break down (page 195)

swarming *v.* form of **swarm:** to gather or live in a large group (page 196)

burrow *n.* a hole in the ground to live in (page 197)

circulate *v.* to flow around freely (page 200)

predator *n.* any animal that lives by hunting another animal for food (page 201)

Practice **Write the vocabulary word next to the group of words that have a similar meaning.**

1. tunnel; hole; den _____burrow_____

2. rots; spoils; decomposes _____decays_____

3. gathering; crowding; thronging _____swarming_____

4. sink; hang; sag _____droop_____

5. hunter; prowler; killer _____predator_____

6. flow; distribute; move _____circulate_____

7. crumbling; fragile; delicate _____brittle_____

8. wrinkle; shrink; diminish _____shrivel_____

Name _____ **Date** _____

Fact and Opinion

Writers use facts and opinions to support ideas in their writing.

- A **fact** is a statement that can be proven true.

  A square has four sides. (You can prove this statement by drawing a square and counting the sides.)

- An **opinion** is what someone feels or believes is true.

  An opinion cannot be proven true or false.

  Blue squares are the best. (This statement cannot be proven true or false. It is a statement about what someone believes.)

Practice A   **Read the following sentences. Ask yourself the question, "Can this sentence be proven true?" If it can be proven true, then it is a fact. Write an X next to each sentence that is a fact.**

1. __X__ A triangle has three sides.

2. _____ The moon is made of cheese.

3. __X__ Cats have paws.

4. __X__ A bicycle has two wheels.

5. _____ All children are noisy.

6. __X__ The Amazon River is in South America.

7. _____ Basketball players are more talented than other athletes.

8. _____ The surface of the sun is very hot.

Name _____ Date _____

Fact and Opinion

Practice B Read the following sentences. Ask yourself the question, "Can this sentence be proven true or false?" If it cannot be proven true or false, then it is an opinion. Write an *O* next to each sentence that is an opinion.

9. _____ Lemons are yellow.

10. __O__ Shoes are better than sandals.

11. __O__ My birthday is the best day of the year.

12. _____ The English language has 26 letters in its alphabet.

13. _____ Orange juice contains vitamin C.

14. __O__ Mary is prettier than Carol.

15. __O__ My computer is better than Kit's.

Read the paragraph below. The paragraph has both facts and opinions. Draw one line under the facts. Draw two lines under the opinions.

    I think aluminum cans are better than plastic bottles. Aluminum is one of the most common elements on this planet. This element makes up about 8 percent of Earth's crust. I believe aluminum cans are better because they come from the planet.

Apply What's your opinion on recycling aluminum cans? Write a sentence stating your opinion. **Answers will vary**

Possible Answer I think it is important to recycle aluminum cans so we don't waste things.

Name _____ Date _____

Antonyms

Antonyms are words that have opposite, or almost opposite, meanings.

• An analogy is two pairs of words that are related in the same way

Example: *night is to day as up is to down*

insult	tragedy	compliment	comedy	proud
unite	ashamed	prey	divide	predator

Practice **Dictionary Strategy**
Choose the spelling word that correctly completes the sentence. Write a sentence using the word that does not fit. Use a dictionary as needed.

1. I was very hurt by the (insult, compliment). _____insult_____

   Sentences will vary. _____

2. I was (proud, ashamed) of the award I received. _____proud_____

   Sentences will vary. _____

3. The lion's (predator, prey) fled as quickly as possible. _____prey_____

   Sentences will vary. _____

4. We laughed throughout the entire (tragedy, comedy). _____comedy_____

   Sentences will vary. _____

5. The couple decided to (unite, divide) in marriage. _____unite_____

   Sentences will vary. _____

Name _____ Date _____

Sentences with Compound Predicates

Focus A **compound predicate** is two or more predicates that have the same subject in a sentence.

Example: The bird **grabbed the twig and flew to its nest.**

Practice Finish each sentence with a compound predicate.

1. The tiny baby _**Possible Answer** cried for five minutes and went to sleep._

2. Joachin _**Possible Answer** put his cleats on and went to soccer practice._

3. The newscaster _**Possible Answer** looked into the camera and started talking._

4. The book I'm reading _**Possible Answer** is two hundred pages long and_ _talks about dinosaurs._

5. My neighbor _**Possible Answer** called me over to her house and gave me a_ _basket of fresh vegetables._

6. Logan's grandma _**Possible Answer** washed her car and cleaned out her_ _garage._

Name _____ **Date** _____

Homographs

Focus

Homographs are words that are spelled the same but have different meanings and different pronunciations.

The judge will permit them to get a parking permit.

To permit means to allow.

A permit is a written warrant or license.

Use these words to complete the exercise below.

house	dwelling	contain
resume	continue	work history
mouth	facial feature	form words
deliberate	intentional	consider
combine	mix together	machine to harvest crops

Practice   **Write the meaning of the underlined word in the sentence.**

1. She needed a place to <u>house</u> her gerbil. _____dwelling_____

2. He handed his <u>resume</u> to the president of the company. _____work history_____

3. The Captain tried to <u>mouth</u> the orders over the roaring waves. _____form words_____

4. Her parents would <u>deliberate</u> about getting her a new bike. _____consider_____

5. The farmer used the <u>combine</u> to get the fields ready for the spring harvest.
   _____machine_____

Name _____   Date _____

Selection Vocabulary

Focus

ancestors *n.* plural of noun ancestor: someone from long ago who is a direct relation to you; for example a great-great-grandparent

pollinate *v.* to spread pollen from flower to flower, allowing fruit and seeds to grow

wither *v.* to dry up; to shrivel

smoldering *adj.* burning and smoking without flames

oxygen *n.* a gas that makes up about one fifth of Earth's atmosphere and that animals must breathe to live

clinging *v.* form of **cling:** to hold on tight

start *n.* a jump due to a surprise

dangle *v.* to hang; to swing loosely

Practice   **Match each word on the left to its definition on the right.**

1. dangle

2. oxygen

3. ancestors

4. pollinate

5. clinging

6. start

7. wither

8. smoldering

a. slowly burning without a fire

b. jumping reaction to being surprised

c. a gas that humans and animals need to survive

d. languish and wilt

e. relatives that lived in the past

f. to carry pollen to flowers from other flowers

g. to swing freely

h. grasping and not letting go

Name _____ **Date** _____

Classifying and Categorizing

Focus Classifying items into categories is a useful way of organizing information.

Classifying means putting similar things into groups or categories. A **category** is the name under which things are grouped. For example, *trumpet, violin, guitar,* and *clarinet* can be classified into the category *Musical Instruments.*

Musical Instruments (*Category*)

trumpet	guitar
violin	clarinet

Some items can fit into more than one category.

Musical Instruments	**Stringed Instruments**
violin	violin
guitar	guitar

Practice A Look at the groups of things below. In each group, two things belong to the same category, but one does not. Write an *X* next to the thing that does not belong with the others.

1. _____ Brazil

   __X__ airplane

   _____ France

2. _____ lemon

   _____ orange

   __X__ triangle

3. _____ daisy

   __X__ whale

   _____ tulip

Name _____ Date _____

Classifying and Categorizing (continued)

 **Practice B**   Look at the groups of things below. Choose a category from the box that best fits each group. Write the category in the space provided.

U.S. Presidents	Sports	Shapes	Tools	Buildings

4. baseball   hockey   soccer

Category: _____**Sports**_____

5. George Washington   Abraham Lincoln   John F. Kennedy

Category: ___**U.S. Presidents**___

6. skyscraper   house   apartment

Category: _____**Buildings**_____

7. hammer   screwdriver   wrench

Category: _____**Tools**_____

8. triangle   rectangle   circle

Category: _____**Shapes**_____

 **Apply**   List two items under each of the following categories.
Possible Answers

Oceans	Flowers	Countries
Pacific Ocean	lilies	Nigeria
Indian Ocean	roses	Japan

Name _____ Date _____

Homographs

Homographs are words that are spelled the same way, but they have different meanings and pronunciations.

record	defect	project	upset	produce
dove	minute	perfect	resent	address

Proofreading Strategy
Circle the misspelled words and write them correctly.

1. (produse,) produce _____produce_____

2. (rekord,) record _____record_____

3. defect, (difekt) _____defect_____

4. (upsett,) upset _____upset_____

5. (progect,) project _____project_____

6. minute, (minit) _____minute_____

7. address, (adress) _____address_____

8. perfect, (prefectt) _____perfect_____

9. (resennt,) resent _____resent_____

10. (dove,) douve _____dove_____

Name _____ Date _____

Coordinating Conjunctions

Focus

A **conjunction** is a word that connects words or groups of words. The words *and, but,* and *or* are **coordinating conjunctions.** They connect related groups of words.

Example: You may either finish your homework **or** go to bed.

Dan may help you, **but** he has other jobs to do too.

Combine two simple sentences by adding a conjunction to form a **compound sentence.**

Example: Zoe ate her lunch. She wasn't really hungry.

Zoe ate her lunch, **but** she wasn't really hungry.

Practice

Join the pairs of sentences below into compound sentences by adding a comma and the conjunction in parentheses.

1. I would like to race motorcycles. My father won't let me. (but)

   I would like to race motorcycles, but my father won't let me.

2. Gigi entered the writing contest. She won first prize. (and)

   Gigi entered the writing contest, and she won first prize.

3. Wesley's dad will pick him up from school. He might ride home with me. (or)

   Wesley's dad will pick him up from school, or he might ride home with me.

4. We picked Ginny up from the airport. She was very grateful. (and)

   We picked Ginny up from the airport, and she was very grateful.

Name _____ Date _____

Greek Roots

Focus Roots carry meaning. Many words in the English language have **Greek roots.** Knowing what a Greek root means helps you to figure out a word's meaning.

Greek roots:

cycl means "circle."

tele means "far off."

logy means "to speak" or "to study."

port means "to carry."

Practice **For each Greek root, write three English words that contain it.**

1. *cycl* **Possible Answers** tricycle, bicycle, unicycle

2. *tele* **Possible Answers** telegram, telephone, telegraph

3. *logy* **Possible Answers** biology, technology, eulogy

4. *port* **Possible Answers** airport, transport, porter

Write the definitions of the following words. You may use a dictionary.

5. eulogy **Possible Answer** a speech given to honor someone who has died.

6. portfolio **Possible Answer** a carrying case for holding papers and drawings.

Name _____ Date _____

Selection Vocabulary

**Focus**

declared *v.* past tense of **declare:** to announce

independence *n.* freedom from the control of another country

original *adj.* first

settle *v.* to decide

contribute *v.* to give money or time

proper *adj.* suitable; correct

violate *v.* to fail to obey; to break

**Practice** **Write the vocabulary word that best matches the underlined word or phrase in the sentences below.**

1. Grandma <u>announced</u> that her new house was ready for overnight guests.

    declared

2. Would you like to <u>give your time or money</u> to the Save-A-Tree Foundation?

    contribute

3. Kohli's mom always makes sure her daughter uses <u>correct</u> manners.

    proper

4. Graham and Andrew need to <u>decide</u> on a location for the campout.

    settle

5. With <u>freedom</u> comes a lot of responsibility. ___independence___

6. My great-great-uncle was one of the <u>first</u> settlers in this town.

    original

Name _____ Date _____

Main Idea and Details

Focus The **main idea** is what a paragraph is about. **Details** in the paragraph support the main idea.

A paragraph has a main idea and details that support the main idea.

- The **main idea** is the most important point the writer makes. The main idea is often stated in a clear topic sentence. The topic sentence is usually at the beginning or the end of a paragraph.

- The other sentences in a paragraph have **details,** or information, that describe the main idea more fully.

Practice A Look at the main idea and details. Write an *X* next to the sentence that more fully describes the main idea.

1. Main idea: A time line shows the order in which things happen.

   __X__ The thing that happened first is always on the left.

   _____ I started the time line with 1970.

   _____ A time line can be fun to make.

2. Main idea: The first colonists came from Spain.

   _____ A fort would be a good thing for a new colony.

   _____ Christopher Columbus traveled in three ships from Spain.

   __X__ They built a colony called St. Augustine.

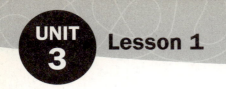
Name _____ Date _____

Main Idea and Details (continued)

Practice B **Read the following paragraph. Then, answer the questions below.**

Ice hockey is one of the fastest of all team sports. Its players race across the rink on ice skates. They swing their sticks to knock a hard rubber puck into the other team's goal. Hockey players are constantly on the move. The game does not stop even when players are substituted. The speed of play results in plenty of rough-and-tumble action.

3. What is this paragraph about? Write the sentence that contains the main idea.

Ice hockey is one of the fastest of all team sports.

_____

4. Now look for sentences with details that support the main idea. Write one sentence that contains details that describe the main idea more fully.

Possible Answer Its players race across the rink on ice skates.

_____

5. Hockey players are constantly on the move. Look at another detail in one of the sentences in the paragraph. How does it describe the main idea more fully? Write the detail and explain.

Possible Answer The game does not stop even when players

are substituted.

_____

Name _____ Date _____

Homophones

Focus   **Homophones** are words that sound alike, but homophones are spelled differently and have different meanings.

Example: *choose* and *chews*

- Understanding the meanings of homophones helps you use the words correctly.

through	threw	passed	past	peace
piece	frees	would	freeze	wood

**Practice**   **Meaning Strategy**
Choose the correct spelling word to complete the sentences.

1. Would you like a (piece, peace) of pie? _____ piece

2. I (wood, would) love to travel around the world. _____ would

3. We went (through, threw) three tunnels and (past, passed) two lakes on

   the way to grandma's house. _____ through, _____ passed

4. I hope it is cold enough for the pond to (frees, freeze). _____ freeze

Write a sentence using each spelling word.
Answers will vary.

5. peace

6. wood

7. threw

8. passed

Name _____ Date _____

Personal Pronouns

Focus

Rule	**Example**
• A **pronoun** is used in place of one or more nouns.	• President Bush said **President Bush** would speak at the university. President Bush said **he** would speak at the university.
	• **Sam and Jamie** met him in Washington, D.C. **They** met him in Washington, D.C.
• When you speak of yourself and someone else, always speak of yourself last.	• **Serena and I** are going to hear President Bush speak.

Practice   **Underline the pronouns in these sentences.**

1. You would enjoy learning about the Pony Express.

2. It was started in 1860.

3. A group of men said that they would deliver mail to the West.

4. Their horseback riders would hand off the mail to another rider.

5. He would then continue the route.

Circle the correct combination.

6. (Sunee and I), I and Sunee) went to the museum today.

Name _____ Date _____

Synonyms

Focus **Synonyms** are words that are similar in meaning.

Practice A Circle the synonym for the word in each line.

1. **smell** (scent, nose)

2. **automobile** (car, train)

3. **fuzzy** (blurry, fast)

4. **incorrect** (right, wrong)

5. **humid** (muggy, dry)

6. **disturb** (bother, help)

7. **split** (divide, sew)

8. **liquid** (lotion, fluid)

Practice B Write a sentence using a synonym for the word *observe*.

Possible Answer Did you notice what he was wearing on his head?

Name _____ Date _____

Selection Vocabulary

Focus
> **colonies** *n.* plural form of **colony:** settlement formed by people who have come to a new land
>
> **skill** *v.* ability to do something
>
> **astronomy** *n.* the science of studying the universe outside the Earth's atmosphere
>
> **positions** *n.* plural form of **position:** place where things are located
>
> **site** *n.* location; place to build
>
> **capital** *adj.* where the government is located

Practice Circle the correct word that completes each sentence.

1. I haven't yet perfected the _____ of dribbling the basketball without looking.
   a. (skill)   **b.** site   **c.** colonies

2. Paulo wants to study _____ when he gets older.
   a. capital   **b.** site   **c.** (astronomy)

3. The _____ for the new restaurant is still under construction.
   a. capital   **b.** positions   **c.** (site)

4. Our drama teacher marked our _____ on the stage with masking tape.
   a. capital   **b.** (positions)   **c.** skill

5. Tennessee was not one of the original _____.
   a. astronomy   **b.** positions   **c.** (colonies)

Name _____ Date _____

Drawing Conclusions

Focus **Drawing conclusions helps readers get more information from a story.**

Here is how you **draw conclusions:**

- Look for bits of information or details about a character or an event in a story. Use these details to make a statement or draw a conclusion about that character or event.

- Sometimes a conclusion is stated in the story. Sometimes it is not. However, a conclusion is always supported by details in the story.

Practice A **Look at the groups of sentences below. The sentences in the first column are details. The sentences in the second column are possible conclusions. One conclusion is correct, and one is incorrect. Put an X next to the sentence that could be the conclusion to the first pair of sentences. The first one is done for you.**

Details

1. Carmen likes all kinds of cheese.

Cheddar is a kind of cheese.

2. Rover is a dog.

All dogs are animals.

3. Tasha plays the cello.

People who play the cello are musicians.

Conclusions

1. __X__ Carmen likes cheddar.

_____ Carmen does not like cheddar.

2. _____ Rover is an elephant.

__X__ Rover is an animal.

3. __X__ Tasha is a musician.

_____ Tasha plays the flute.

Name _____ Date _____

Drawing Conclusions

Practice B   Read the paragraph. Then answer the following.

Marta hung her favorite red jacket on the hook behind the closet door. Roberta, Marta's younger sister, liked the red jacket as much as Marta.

"May I wear your red jacket today?" Roberta asked.

"Not today," Marta replied, "I will need to wear it later this evening. I'm sorry."

Marta left the bedroom and went downstairs to finish her chores. Roberta pouted and folded her arms in front of her. Roberta was disappointed.

She said to herself, reaching for the jacket, "I just want to wear the jacket to the park for a couple of hours."

Several hours later, Marta returned to the bedroom to get her jacket. She gasped. Her favorite red jacket was covered with a fresh layer of mud!

4. The sentences in this paragraph contain many details. One detail is that Roberta asks Marta for permission to wear Marta's jacket. Write two more details you find in this paragraph.

   Detail: **Possible Answer** Roberta was disappointed. _____

   Detail: **Possible Answer** The jacket was covered with mud. _____

5. Judging by the details in this paragraph, what can you conclude?
   Possible Answer Roberta wore Marta's jacket to the park and got it covered

   with mud. _____

Name _____ **Date** _____

Homonyms and Homophones

Focus **Homonyms** and **homophones** are words that sound alike.

• Homonyms are words that are spelled the same and sound the same but have different meanings.

• Homophones are words that sound the same but have different spellings and meanings.

• Many words have more than one meaning. Understanding the different meanings of words helps you use them correctly.

pitcher	spring	swallow	bark	train
splinter	stalk	change	uniform	vault

Practice **Meaning Strategy**
Write the spelling word next to the clue. Write a sentence using the word in another way. Use a dictionary as needed.

1. a kind of bird _____swallow_____

Sentences will vary. _____

2. money that is left over _____change_____

Sentences will vary. _____

3. a part of a plant _____stalk_____

Sentences will vary. _____

4. the covering on a tree _____bark_____

Sentences will vary. _____

Name _____ Date _____

Relative and Demonstrative Pronouns

Focus

A **relative pronoun** introduces a part of a sentence, or clause, which describes a noun. A relative pronoun *relates* to another noun that comes before it in a sentence. There are five main relative pronouns: *that, which, who, whom,* and *whose.*

A **demonstrative pronoun** points out a particular person, place, or thing. *This* and *these* refer to people, places, or things that are nearby. *That* and *those* usually refer to people, places, or things that are farther away.

Practice A

Fill in the blank with a relative or demonstrative pronoun.

1. The author wrote a book _____*that*_____ explained how to play hockey.

2. _____*Those*_____ papers are over on my desk.

3. Tami is the one _____*who*_____ asked for help.

4. _____*This*_____ chair I'm sitting on was just painted yesterday.

5. Can you help me find the girl _____*whose*_____ gloves these are?

6. I've seen _____*that*_____ bright star every night this week.

Practice B

Write a sentence using a demonstrative pronoun describing something far away.

Possible Answer I saw a giant tortoise in that habitat on the other side of the zoo.

Name _____ Date _____

Latin Roots

 **Focus**   The words *platform, uniform, transform, reform,* and *inform* contain the **Latin root** *form.*

The **Latin root** *form* means "shape."

Oftentimes, knowing the meaning of a root will help you figure out the meanings of unfamiliar words.

Practice   **Read the following sentences and write the meanings of the underlined words.**

1. The president stood on the <u>platform</u> as he read his speech to the crowd.

Possible Answer a raised surface
_____

2. Our <u>uniforms</u> were in great shape at the beginning of the year.

Possible Answer clothing that is the same
_____

3. The decorator will <u>transform</u> the appearance of the hall.

Possible Answer to change in appearance
_____

4. The grinch promised to <u>reform</u> his ways. He will no longer be mean to children.

Possible Answer to make or change for better
_____

5. The principal told us to <u>inform</u> our parents that our school will be closed tomorrow.

Possible Answer to tell
_____

Name _____ Date _____

Selection Vocabulary

Focus

rumors *n.* stories without proof that pass from person to person

distract *v.* to draw attention away from what someone is doing

deserted *v.* past tense of **desert:** to leave; abandon

impressed *v.* past tense of **impress:** to have a strong effect on someone's feelings

abundance *n.* a large amount

elegant *adj.* rich and fine in quality

typical *adj.* average; normal for its kind

Practice Write T in the blank if the sentence for the vocabulary word is correct. Write F if the sentence is false. For each F answer, write the word that fits the definition.

1. If something is *deserted,* it is abandoned.

__T__ _____

2. If something is *elegant,* it is common.

__F__ ____typical____

3. If you *distract* someone, you divert their attention to something else.

__T__ _____

4. *Abundance* means "plenty of."

__T__ _____

Name _____ **Date** _____

Comparatives

Focus The suffix *-er* means "more."

• **Comparatives** that end in *-er* are used to compare two things. Sometimes you need to make spelling changes to the base word when you add *-er*.

• When words end in *y*, change the *y* to an *i* and then add *-er*.

• In some cases the final consonant doubles when *-er* is added.

harder	freer	thinner	scarier	truer
cuter	dimmer	bolder	nicer	calmer

Practice **Conventions Strategy**
Add the suffix *-er* to each base to form a spelling word. Remember, you may need to change the base word before adding the suffix.

1. hard + er = _____harder_____
2. calm + er = _____calmer_____
3. dim + er = _____dimmer_____
4. thin + er = _____thinner_____
5. cute + er = _____cuter_____

6. true + er = _____truer_____
7. scary + er = _____scarier_____
8. free + er = _____freer_____
9. nice + er = _____nicer_____
10. bold + er = _____bolder_____

Name _____ Date _____

Superlative Adjectives

 **Focus** **Superlative adjectives** compare three or more things. Superlative forms of most one-syllable adjectives end in *-est*.

Example: Prina is the *tallest* girl in her class.

Add the word *most* to most adjectives with two or more syllables to form their superlatives.

Example: The test was the *most challenging* I've ever taken.

 **Practice** **Circle the correct superlative adjective in parentheses.**

1. I think the blue butterfly is the (beautifulest/(most beautiful)) one.

2. My grandma is the (caringest/(most caring)) person I know.

3. The turtle is one of the ((slowest)/most slow) animals on earth.

4. That star is definitely the ((brightest)/most bright) in the sky.

5. My mom is the (carefulest/(most careful)) driver in our family.

6. Our basement is the ((darkest)/most dark) room in our house.

Grammar, Usage and Mechanics • *Reteach*

Name _____   Date _____

Greek Roots

Focus   **Roots** carry meaning. Many words in the English language have **Greek roots.** Knowing what a Greek root means helps you to figure out a word's meaning

Greek roots

path means "feeling."

mim means "to copy or imitate."

opt means "eye."

ortho means "straight."

cycl means "circle."

tele means "far off."

logy means "to speak."

port means "to carry."

Practice A   **For each Greek root, write two English words that contain it.**

1. path   **Possible Answer** pathetic, empathy

2. tele   **Possible Answer** telegram, telephone

3. opt   **Possible Answer** optical, optometry

4. ortho   **Possible Answer** orthotics, orthodontist

Practice B   **Write a definition for the following word. Check a dictionary to see if your guess was correct.**

5. empathy **Possible Answer** Understanding and identifying with someone's

feelings

Name _____ Date _____

Selection Vocabulary

Focus
    associations *n.* plural of **association:** a friendship and connection

    detained *v.* form of **detain:** keep back

vast *adj.* large; widespread

engaged *v.* busy with

tremendous *adj.* very large

provisions *n.* a supply of food and other necessary items

permanent *adj.* lasting; not temporary

Practice   **Fill in each blank with a vocabulary word from this lesson to complete each sentence.**

1. Della has a lot of ___associations___ at other schools.

2. The prairie, stretching for miles, is so open and ___vast___.

3. I have a ___tremendous___ amount of homework tonight.

4. Brianna brought enough ___provisions___ for our entire troop.

5. Is this your ___permanent___ address, or will you be moving again soon?

6. The teacher ___detained___ Silvia after school.

7. Will you be ___engaged___ with your science project all weekend?

Name _____ Date _____

Superlatives

The suffix -*est* means "most."

- **Superlatives** that end in -*est* are used to compare many things.
- Sometimes you need to make spelling changes to the base word when you add -*est*.
- For words that end in e, just add -*st*.
- For words that end in y, change the y to i before adding -*est*.
- In some cases, the final consonant doubles when -*est* is added.

hottest **fittest**	**fanciest** **smoothest**	**noblest** **clumsiest**	**fullest** **dearest**	**heaviest** **sharpest**

Conventions Strategy
Add the suffix -est to the words to form spelling words. Remember you may need to change the base word before adding the suffix.

1. hot   + est = ___hottest___

2. sharp   + est = ___sharpest___

3. smooth + est = ___smoothest___

4. full   + est = ___fullest___

5. fancy   + est = ___fanciest___

6. dear   + est = ___dearest___

7. clumsy + est = ___clumsiest___

8. noble   + est = ___noblest___

9. heavy   + est = ___heaviest___

10. fit   + est = ___fittest___

Name _____ Date _____

Comparative Adjectives

Focus

A **comparative adjective** compares two things.

Comparative adjectives add -er to most one-syllable adjectives. Use *more* in front of most adjectives with two or more syllables, but do not add -er to the end of the adjective.

Examples:

Lizette's bike is *larger* than mine.

My bike is *more colorful* than Lizette's.

Practice

Read the paragraph. Circle the correct comparative adjective in each set of parentheses.

Laina and E. J. competed against each other in the obstacle course. They were very evenly matched. Laina was (more fast/(faster)) running through the cones. Then E. J. had a (gooder/(better)) time through the tires. They both messed up a little on the ropes, but Laina's mistake was ((bigger)/more big). E. J. fell off the monkey bars once, but Laina was ((more careful)/carefuller). In the end, E. J. proved to be the (more speedy/(speedier)) of the two girls.

Name _____ Date _____

Contractions

Focus A **contraction** is a shortened form of two words. It is formed by combining two words and leaving out one or more letters. It includes an apostrophe to show where the letter or letters have been left out.

Example:

they will = they'll

it is = it's

will not = won't

did not = didn't

we have = we've

Practice A Combine each of the following word pairs to make a contraction.

1. we would _____ we'd _____

2. you are _____ you're _____

3. they had _____ they'd _____

4. can not _____ can't _____

5. it has _____ it's _____

Practice B Write a sentence using one of the contractions you formed above.

6. **Possible Answer** I'd like to see your photo album sometime.
   _____

Name _____ Date _____

Selection Vocabulary

Focus

politics *n.* the activity of government and running for offices

legislator *n.* a member of the part of government that makes laws

debates *n.* plural of **debate**: a public discussion of issues by people who disagree

intelligence *n.* the ability to think, learn, and understand

rebelling *v.* form of **rebel**: to fight against authority

liberty *n.* freedom to act, think, or speak as one pleases

Practice   **Review the vocabulary words and definitions from "Abraham Lincoln: Sixteenth President." Write two sentences that each use at least one of the vocabulary words.**

1. **Possible Answer** Isa may only be eight, but she is already very interested in politics.

2. **Possible Answer** Benito is intrigued by chimpanzees and their intelligence.

Name _____ **Date** _____

Contractions

Focus

A **contraction** is a shortened form of two words.

- When the words are joined together, an apostrophe is used to take the place of at least one letter or word.

- Some contractions look the same, but have different possible meanings.

I'm	don't	he'll	it's	can't
they'd	we'll	you'd	o'clock	we'd

Practice

Conventions Strategy
Write a spelling word to replace the boldface words.

1. **I am** going to see my friend. ___I'm___

2. I **do not** like squash unless **it is** cooked. ___don't,___ ___it's___

3. **We will** leave at 6 **of the clock.** ___we'll,___ ___o'clock___

4. **They would** be happy if **you would** come, too. ___they'd,___ ___you'd___

5. **He will** be at the party, but he **can not** stay long. ___he'll,___ ___can't___

6. **We had** better rest before the big hike. ___we'd___

Name _____   Date _____

Comparative and Superlative Adverbs

Focus   **Comparative adverbs** compare two actions.

To form comparative adverbs, add *-er* to most one-syllable adverbs and use *more* with most adverbs with two or more syllables.

Superlative adverbs compare three or more actions.

To make superlative adverbs, add *-est* to most one-syllable adverbs. Use *most* with many adverbs that have two or more syllables.

Practice   **Circle the correct adverb form in parentheses.**

1. Of the three runners, Candice was moving (more slowly/most slowly).

2. Both boys looked happy, but Jimmy was grinning (more widely/most widely).

3. Kohli bowed (more dramatically/most dramatically) than the other girls.

4. Of the three cars, Aidan's moved (more swiftly/most swiftly).

5. My brother cleaned his room (more thoroughly/most thoroughly) than he did last week.

6. That stinkweed plant smells the (worse/worst) of all.

Name _____ Date _____

Root Plus Suffixes *-ic, -ly, -ist, -er*

Focus

A **suffix** is an addition to the end of a word (brea*king*).

A **root word** is a word to which a suffix can be added (*break*ing).

Adding the suffix **-ly** to the end of words changes adjectives to adverbs, which describe the way something occurs. Example: *easily*

The suffix *-ly* also changes root words that are nouns into adjectives. Example: *motherly*

The suffix **-ic** means "having to do with." The root word changes from a noun to an adjective when this suffix is added. Example: *heroic*

The suffix **-ist** means "one who practices." In this case, the part of speech of the root word does not change. Example: *biologist*

The suffix **-er** changes verbs to nouns. Example: *shopper*

Practice

Change the words to the parts of speech in parentheses by adding a suffix (*-ly, -ic, -ist, -er*)

1. swift (adverb) _____swiftly_____

2. scholar (adjective) _____scholarly_____

3. drive (noun) _____driver_____

4. metal (adjective) _____metallic_____

5. botany (noun) _____botanist_____

6. slow (adverb) _____slowly_____

7. history (adjective) _____historic_____

8. dive (noun) _____diver_____

Name _____ Date _____

Selection Vocabulary

Focus

crabbier *adj.* form of **crabby:** cross; in a bad mood

local *adj.* nearby

observations *n.* plural of **observation:** an act of noticing something

examine *v.* to look closely

results *n.* plural of **result:** what you find out when you do an experiment

certain *adj.* sure

react *v.* to act because something has happened

anxious *adj.* eager

Practice **Write the vocabulary word next to the group of words that have a similar meaning.**

1. outcomes; effects; consequences _____results_____

2. respond; act again; move _____react_____

3. nervous; excited; anticipating _____anxious_____

4. positive; without a doubt; assured _____certain_____

5. not far away; near; close _____local_____

6. things seen; details noticed; examinations _____observations_____

7. observe; see; look _____examine_____

8. grumpier; grouchier; more irritated _____crabbier_____

Name _____ Date _____

Suffixes

Focus When suffixes are added to root words, the meaning of the root word changes.

- *-ity* changes an adjective into a noun.
- *-al* changes a noun into an adjective.
- *-less* means "without."
- *-or* means "a person with–____."
- *-ly* means "in a ____ way."

locality	briskly	oddity	properly	flavorless
critical	needless	digital	inspector	editor

Practice **Visualization Strategy**
Fill in the missing letters and write the spelling word.

1. ed_i_t_o_r   editor

2. l_oca_l_i_ty   locality

3. pr_op_erly   properly

4. br_i_skly   briskly

5. fl_a_v_o_rl_e_ss   flavorless

6. ne_ed_l_e_ss   needless

7. cr_it_ical   critical

8. d_ig_ital   digital

9. _o_dd_i_ty   oddity

10. _i_nsp_e_ct_o_r   inspector

Name _____ Date _____

Regular Verbs

Focus

Regular verbs are verbs that follow a certain pattern when they change tenses.

Talk is a regular verb.

They *talk.* She *talked.*

Talk and *talked* are forms of the verb *to talk. Talk* shows an action currently happening, while *talked* shows an action in the past.

If the subject of a sentence is singular, most verbs add -s or -es to create the present tense, but add nothing for plural subjects.

To form the past tense, add -ed to the verb.

Practice Change each verb to the tense in parentheses, and write it in a sentence.

1. **shouted** (present) **Possible Answer** They shout with excitement whenever their team scores.

2. **twirl** (past) **Possible Answer** Gretchen twirled around the bedroom in her new skirt.

3. **interrupt** (past) **Possible Answer** Nolan interrupted the teacher while she was talking.

4. **appeared** (present) **Possible Answer** Our neighbor's dogs appear in our backyard every time we cook on the grill.

5. **clean** (past) **Possible Answer** Cici cleaned Heather's room for her.

Name _____ **Date** _____

Roots Plus Prefixes *mis-, un-, dis-, and im-*

Focus The prefixes **mis-, un-, dis-** and **im-** all have a similar meaning: *not,* or *opposite.*

Examples: *mis*fortune, *un*happy, *dis*agree, *im*possible

Practice **Circle the correct word in parentheses.**

1. It is (unlikely/mislikely) that we will have recess outside in the rain.

2. Asha thinks her little brother is (unmature/immature).

3. The cast on Nicki's arm is causing her (discomfort/miscomfort).

4. Deklan (unspelled/misspelled) the word "catastrophe" in the spelling bee.

5. We are studying (unproper/improper) fractions in math class.

6. The product has been (uncontinued/discontinued) due to safety concerns.

7. Sharing your snack with a friend is a very (unselfish/misselfish) thing to do.

8. The repairman had to (misconnect/disconnect) our phone line while he worked on it.

Name _____ **Date** _____

Selection Vocabulary

Focus

attract *v.* to cause something to come closer

pure *adj.* not mixed with anything

rarely *adv.* not often

force *n.* the push or pull of something

core *n.* the central, most important, or inner part of something

related *adj.* connected

current *n.* flow of electricity

friction *n.* the rubbing of one thing against another

Practice Match each word on the left to its definition on the right.

1. current

2. related

3. force

4. core

5. pure

6. friction

7. attract

8. rarely

a. how much something is moving against another object

b. uncontaminated

c. having to do with each other

d. rubbing back and forth

e. the inside of something

f. hardly ever

g. jolt of electric shock

h. make something come near

Name _____ Date _____

Prefixes

Focus

When prefixes are added to root words, the meaning of the root word changes.

- *de-* means "take away, or do the opposite."
- *im-* means "not."
- *pre-* means "before."
- *co-* means "together, with."
- *en-* means "to cause to be."

| immobile | enforce | demerit | enrich | declaw |
| copilot | impolite | costar | prefix | preschool |

Practice

Conventions Strategy
Add the prefix to form a spelling word.

1. de + claw = _declaw_
2. co + star = _costar_
3. en + force = _enforce_
4. en + rich = _enrich_
5. pre + fix = _prefix_

6. im + mobile = _immobile_
7. im + polite = _impolite_
8. co + pilot = _copilot_
9. de + school = _demerit_
10. pre + merit = _preschool_

Name _____   Date _____

Irregular Verbs

Focus   Came/Come, Rang/Rung, Sang/Sung, Took/Taken, Gave/Given, Ate/Eaten, Went/Gone

Read the paragraph. Correct any underlined verbs that are incorrect. Use proofreading marks to make the corrections.

The doorbell had rang. The pizza was finally here.   rung
Melissa's friends felt like they hadn't ate in hours even   eaten
though they had been given plenty of food. Melissa told   correct
her parents that she had went to check on Tony, and it   gone
sounded like he had sang himself to sleep. Her mother   sung
had came into the room to get a piece of pizza. She was   come
surprised by what Melissa said, because Tony never taken   took
a nap unless he was very tired. When she went down the   correct
hall to Tony's room to check on him, her husband came   correct
with her.

Practice   Went/Gone, Took/Taken, Gave/Given, Sang/Sung

Read the paragraph. Circle the correct verb in parentheses.

"Where did Tony go?" Melissa's father asked.

"I'm not sure where he (gone, (went))," her mother
answered, "but Melissa said he was tired after he (sung,
(sang)) that song for her friends. Maybe he (taken, (took))
his blanket with him and has ((gone), went) to his room to
rest."

"He hasn't let that blanket out of his sight ever since
Melissa (given, (gave)) it to him for his birthday last year."

"I know. Melissa had ((taken), took) it away from him
once so she could wash it, but Tony got so upset that she
((gave), given) it right back."

Name _____ **Date** _____

Suffixes

> **Focus**   The **suffix** spelling of a base word sometimes changes when a suffix is attached to it.
>
> Sometimes the consonant at the end is doubled before the suffix is added.
>
> Example: *map, mapped*
>
> Sometimes the final *e* is removed before adding the *-ing* ending.
>
> Example: *share, sharing*
>
> Sometimes a final *y* is changed to *i* before adding a suffix.
>
> Example: *easy, easiest*
>
> Sometimes the base word doesn't change at all when a suffix is added.
>
> Example: *great, greater*

Practice   **Add the suffix to the base word. Make any necessary changes. Write the new word on the line.**

1. change   +   ing   =   _changing_

2. borrow   +   ed   =   _borrowed_

3. glide   +   ing   =   _gliding_

4. swat   +   ed   =   _swatted_

5. fry   +   ed   =   _fried_

6. happy   +   est   =   _happiest_

7. cold   +   er   =   _colder_

8. grab   +   ing   =   _grabbing_

Name _____ Date _____

Selection Vocabulary

pursuit *n.* the act of chasing

drizzly *adj.* slightly rainy

findings *n.* plural of **finding:** the results of an investigation

overwhelm *v.* to overpower; to make helpless

competitor *n.* someone selling goods or services in the same market as another person

techniques *n.* plural of **technique:** method; way of doing thing

peered *v.* past tense of **peer:** to look closely

environment *n.* surroundings

Practice **Fill in the blank with a vocabulary word from this lesson to complete each sentence.**

1. Drake tried several different ___techniques___ before he came up with one that worked.

2. I am not sure if those turtles will survive in their new ___environment___.

3. The little girl ___peered___ nervously around her mother at the teacher.

4. The police officers were in ___pursuit___ of the thief.

5. Georgie and Lew conducted the same experiment, but their ___findings___ were very different.

6. I don't think our soccer game will be cancelled due to the ___drizzly___ weather.

7. Lions are so large and fearsome that they ___overwhelm___ their smaller prey.

8. Jamison Elementary is our ___competitor___ in the community fundraiser.

Vocabulary • *Reteach*

Name _____ **Date** _____

Classify and Categorize

Focus Classifying items into categories is a useful way of organizing information.

Classifying means putting similar things into groups or categories. A **category** is the name under which the things are grouped.

Kinds of Transportation *(Category)*

horse, wagon, airplane, car

Some items can fit into more than one category.

Kinds of Transportation		**Modern Transportation**	
airplane	car	airplane	car

Practice A Look at the groups of things below. All the things belong to the same category except one. Write an *X* next to the thing that does not belong in the same category as the others.

1. _____ broccoli   _____ carrot

   _X_ oatmeal   _____ celery

2. _____ poodle   _X_ tiger

   _____ cocker spaniel   _____ German shepherd

3. _X_ hair   _____ table

   _____ chair   _____ sofa

4. _____ maple tree   _X_ coat rack

   _____ palm tree   _____ oak tree

 **Lesson 3**

Name _____ **Date** _____

Classify and Categorize

Practice B   Look at the groups of things below. Choose a category from the box that best fits each group. Write the category in the space provided.

Clothing Colors	Papers Games

5. Category: ____Games____
checkers
chess
tic-tac-toe

6. Category: ____Clothing____
hat
shirt
dress

7. Category: ____Colors____
red
blue
yellow

8. Category: ____Papers____
construction paper
typing paper
tracing paper

   **List two things for each of the following categories.**
Possible Answer

Movies	Sports	Holidays
Annie	Baseball	Halloween
Mary Poppins	Basketball	Thanksgiving

Comprehension Skill • *Reteach*

Spelling Changes with Suffixes

Focus

Sometimes the spelling of a base word changes when you add a suffix. Many words change in predictable ways. Some changes are less predictable.

- If a word ends in e and the ending begins with a vowel, the e is dropped.

drizzly	cautious	nervous	terribly	juror
mobility	supplement	argument	diversion	collision

Practice

Conventions Strategy
Add a suffix to each word to form a spelling word. You may need to change the base word before adding the suffix.

1. drizzle   drizzly

2. argue   argument

3. caution   cautious

4. collide   collision

5. diverse   diversion

6. nerve   nervous

7. jury   juror

8. terrible   terribly

9. mobile   mobility

10. supply   supplement

Name _____   Date _____

Subject and Verb Agreement

Focus

Rule
- A **singular subject** has a verb that agrees in number.
- A **plural subject** has a verb that agrees in number.

Example
- Paul walks.
- Joan runs.
- The senators applaud.
- The children stand.

Practice In the blanks below, write the verb in parentheses that correctly completes each sentence.

1. Wynton Marsalis (play, plays) _____ plays _____ the trumpet.

2. His father and brothers (was, were) _____ were _____ all jazz musicians.

Complete each sentence with a verb that makes sense. Make sure the subject and the verb agree in number.
Answers will vary. Possible Answers are shown.

3. Boris Becker and Pete Sampras _____ play _____ tennis.

4. Weathering _____ changes _____ the surface of Earth.

Think of a person whom you admire. Write a paragraph about some of the things you admire about this person. Make sure the subject and verb in each of your sentences agree in number. Use a separate sheet of paper if you need more space.   Answers will vary.

Possible Answer I admire Abraham Lincoln. He never quit. Even when he failed at

something the first time, he always tried again. He grew up poor. He didn't have

a lot of advantages. People told him he would not amount to much. He became

a great man who did a lot for our country.

Name _____ **Date** _____

Inflectional Endings

Focus | **Inflectional endings** are endings that change the tense of a verb or change a singular noun to a plural noun.

Examples: *-ed, -ing, -s*

Sometimes the consonant at the end is doubled before the suffix is added.

Example: *mop, mopped*

Sometimes the final *e* is removed before adding the *-ing* or *-ed* endings.

Example: *blaze, blazing*

Sometimes a final *y* is changed to *i* before adding a suffix.

Example: *beauty, beauties*

Practice | Add the inflectional ending in parentheses to the bold-faced word. Write the new word in a sentence.

1. **strike** (ing) _Possible Answer She keeps striking the piñata, but it won't break._

2. **flap** (ed) _Possible Answer The bird flapped its wings and flew away._

3. **drag** (ing) _Possible Answer My dog has been dragging that bone around all day._

4. **family** (s) _Possible Answer I have two very different families._

5. **grade** (ed) _Possible Answer I graded Pela's paper, and he graded mine._

6. **step** (s) _Possible Answer Mina climbed up all 150 steps._

Name _____ Date _____

Selection Vocabulary

eclipse *n.* a darkening or hiding of the sun by the moon or of the moon by Earth's shadow

inventions *n.* plural of **invention:** a thing that is made or thought of for the first time

charted *v.* past tense of **chart:** to make a map

forecasts *n.* plural of **forecast:** a prediction about what will happen based on evidence

charge *n.* a load of electricity

shocked *v.* past tense of **shock:** to jolt with electricity

genuine *adj.* real; true

mast *n.* a pole that holds sails

Practice Review the vocabulary words and definitions from "How Ben Franklin Stole the Lightning." Write two sentences that each use at least one of the vocabulary words.

1. **Possible Answer** I don't always believe weather forecasts, because they aren't accurate every time.

2. **Possible Answer** I am not sure if the ring I found has a genuine diamond on it or a fake one.

Name _____   Date _____

Main Idea and Details

Focus

The main idea is what a paragraph is about. Details in the paragraph support the main idea.

A paragraph has a main idea and details that support the main idea.

- The **main idea** is the most important point the writer makes. The main idea is often stated in a clear topic sentence. The topic sentence is usually at the beginning or the end of a paragraph.

- The other sentences in a paragraph have **details,** or information, that describe the main idea more fully.

Practice A   Write an *X* next to the sentence that does not more fully describe the main idea.

1. Main idea: Washington, D.C., became the capital of the United States in 1800.

   __X__ Many cities were named after George Washington.

   _____ It was especially designed to be the capital.

   _____ It was named after George Washington.

2. Main idea: Blind people read with their fingers using Braille, a system of raised dots.

   _____ Braille was developed by Louis Braille in France in 1826 when he was a teenager.

   _____ The Braille alphabet, numbers, punctuation, and speech sounds are represented by 63 different combinations of 6 raised dots arranged in a rectangular shape.

   __X__ I have seen Braille in elevators to represent the floor number.

Name _____ Date _____

Main Idea and Details (Continued)

Practice B Read the following paragraph. Then, answer the questions below.

Birds of prey, also called raptors, are powerful hunters of the sky. There are about 280 different kinds, including eagles, falcons, hawks, owls, and vultures. They all have extremely sharp eyesight. They can spot their prey on the ground from a great height. Raptors have long, strong legs with sharp claws, called talons, for grasping their victims.

Answers will vary. Possible answers are shown.

3. What is this paragraph about? Write the sentence that contains the main idea.

Birds of prey, also called raptors, are powerful hunters of the sky.

4. Now look for sentences with details that support the main idea. Write one sentence that contains details that describe the main idea more fully.

Possible Answer They can spot their prey on the ground from a great height.

Apply Look at the following paragraph. The main idea is missing. Based on the details in the sentences, write the main idea of this paragraph.

Food keeps us warm, gives us energy, and helps us grow. Our daily pattern of eating and drinking is called our diet. Lack of the right kinds of food can lead to disease, inadequate growth, and eventually starvation. Eating too much of the wrong kinds of food can cause heart disease and other illnesses.

Answers will vary. Possible answers are shown.

Possible Answer All living things need food.

Name _____   Date _____

Inflectional Endings -ed and -ing

Focus

The inflectional endings **-ed** and **-ing** usually tell when an action *happened*, or is *happening*.

- Sometimes the spelling of a base word changes when you add an inflectional ending. Changes in the base words usually follow familiar patterns.
- If a word ends in *e*, the *e* is dropped.
- If a word ends in *consonant-y*, the *y* becomes *i*.
- If a word ends in *short vowel-consonant*, double the *consonant*.

charted equipped	daring bowling	shocked controlling	crying cried	amusing dried

Practice

Conventions Strategy
Add -ed or -ing to form spelling words. Remember, you may need to change the base word first.

-ed

1. chart _____charted_____
2. shock _____shocked_____
3. equip _____equipped_____
4. cry _____cried_____
5. dry _____dried_____

-ing

6. dare _____daring_____
7. bowl _____bowling_____
8. control _____controlling_____
9. cry _____crying_____
10. amuse _____amusing_____

Name _____ Date _____

Compound Words

Focus

Compound words are made by joining two whole words. The two words do not necessarily keep the same meanings they had as individual words.

In an **open compound,** the words are not combined into one word.

In a **closed compound,** the two words are joined without a hyphen.

Practice

Circle the compound word in each sentence. Then, write a definition for the word.

1. Bob and Sue just met their first (grandchild) for the first time.

   Possible Answer a child born to your children

2. My dad bought some (fireworks) for our party tonight.

   Possible Answer explosives that make colors and noise

3. My aunt is teaching me (sign language). **Possible Answer** communicating

4. I share a (bedroom) with my older brother. **Possible Answer** a room where you sleep

5. When Grandpa carved the turkey, he gave Jake and me the (wishbone).

   Possible Answer a bone from a bird that is broken for good luck

6. California is on the coast, but South Dakota is (landlocked).

   Possible Answer surrounded by land on all sides

Name _____ Date _____

Selection Vocabulary

Focus

major *adj.* important

common *adj.* happening often; familiar

previous *adj.* earlier

randomly *adv.* by chance

questionnaire *n.* a printed list of questions used by researchers

pace *n.* rate; speed

publication *n.* printed material for the public to read

rejected *v.* past tense of **reject:** to turn down

Practice **Circle the correct word that completes each sentence.**

1. Liam didn't know the _____ owners of the secondhand bike he bought.
   a. pace   **b.** (previous)   **c.** rejected

2. That little yellow car will set the _____ for the race.
   a. publication   **b.** common   **c.** (pace)

3. The winner of the drawing was selected _____.
   a. (randomly)   **b.** previous   **c.** common

4. Our teacher handed us a _____ to fill out about our interests.
   a. pace   **b.** randomly   **c.** (questionnaire)

5. Maury submitted his article for _____.
   a. (publication)   **b.** rejected   **c.** randomly

6. I offered to help Jose, but he _____ my assistance.
   a. common   **b.** pace   **c.** (rejected)

Name _____ Date _____

Author's Purpose

Focus
Writers have reasons for presenting a story in a certain way.

The **author's purpose** is the main reason for presenting a story or selection in a certain way. An author's purpose

- can be to *inform,* to *explain,* to *entertain,* or to *persuade.*
- affects things in the story, such as the *details, descriptions, story events,* and *dialogue.*

An author can have more than one purpose for writing.

Practice A
Read the title of each story below. Then, write what the author's purpose might be for writing the story: *to inform, to explain, to entertain,* **or** *to persuade.*

1. *The Googly-Eyed Monster that Ate Pittsburgh*

Author's Purpose: _____to entertain_____

2. *Building Birdhouses*

Author's Purpose: _____to explain_____

3. *Why Recycling is for Everyone*

Author's Purpose: _____to persuade_____

4. *Miss Bop and the Runaway Flip-Flop*

Author's Purpose: _____to entertain_____

Name _____ Date _____

Author's Purpose

Practice B Using the following topic "Life in California," think of four different essays you could write. Each essay should have a specific purpose. Give each essay a title and briefly explain what it would be about.

Essay #1 (to inform)

Title: **Possible Answer** "The California Gold Rush" _____

Summary: **Possible Answer** I would give dates, places, and other facts about the Gold Rush of 1848.

Essay #2 (to explain)

Title: **Possible Answer** "Finding Your Way Around San Francisco" _____

Summary: **Possible Answer** I would explain to tourists where things are located in San Francisco and how to get from place to place.

Essay #3 (to entertain)

Title: **Possible Answer** "Dax and Davey's Day at the Beach" _____

Summary: **Possible Answer** I would tell a funny story about two boys who go to the beach and take a ride on a whale.

Essay #4 (to persuade)

Title: **Possible Answer** "Take Time to Vote" _____

Summary: **Possible Answer** I would try to convince Californians how important it is to vote on Election Day.

Name _____ Date _____

Compound Words

Focus | **Compound words** are made by combining two smaller words.

| everyone | townhouse | sideways | wheelchair | laptop |
| rainbow | playground | yearbook | bathtub | keyboard |

Practice | **Compound Strategy**
Write two words together to form a compound spelling word.

1. every + one = <u>everyone</u>

2. lap + top = <u>laptop</u>

3. town + house = <u>townhouse</u>

4. wheel + chair = <u>wheelchair</u>

5. rain + bow = <u>rainbow</u>

6. year + book = <u>yearbook</u>

7. key + board = <u>keyboard</u>

8. play + ground = <u>playground</u>

9. bath + tub = <u>bathtub</u>

10. side + ways = <u>sideways</u>

Name _____ Date _____

Correcting Run-ons and Fragments

Focus

Rule	Example
• A group of words that is written as a sentence but is missing a subject or a predicate or both is a **fragment.**	• The president of France
• A sentence with no punctuation or coordinating conjunction between two independent clauses is a **run-on sentence.**	• Every day we use our senses they help us experience the world.
• A **rambling** sentence strings together many thoughts.	• We read about our senses and we asked questions and then we looked through a microscope.
• An **awkward** sentence is a sentence that does not sound or read well.	• Being that we use our senses every day we should protect them because they're ours.

Practice

Read the sentences. Write *fragment, run-on,* or *rambling* in the blank.

1. Clara Barton was born in Massachusetts and she was educated at home and

she worked as a nurse during the Civil War. _____rambling_____

2. Between 1869 and 1873. _____fragment_____

3. She lived in Europe she helped start hospitals during the-Franco-Prussian

War. _____run-on_____

Name _____ Date _____

Greek Roots

Focus Because so many English words come from the Greek, knowing **Greek roots** will help you to decode such words.

Here are some common Greek roots and their meanings

logy = "science of" or "to speak"   *eco* = "environment"

geo = "earth"   *graph* = "write"

opt = "eye"   *photo* = "light"

mim = "to copy or imitate"   *tech* = "art" or "skillful"

ant = "against"   *cycl* = "circle"

path = "feeling"   *scope* = "look at"

Practice Based on what you know about English words that come from Greek, match the following words on the left with their definitions on the right.

1. mimeograph_____ **a.** a duplicating machine

2. optometrist **b.** causing someone to feel emotion for you

3. antonym **c.** one animal imitating another

4. mimicry **d.** a word that means the opposite of another word

5. pathetic **e.** an actor who copies someone else using only gestures

6. mime **f.** eye doctor

Name _____ Date _____

Selection Vocabulary

Focus

buzzing *v.* form of **buzz:** to be very active

ceremony *n.* a formal event, often with speech making

transcontinental *adj.* stretching from coast to coast

laborers *n.* plural of **laborer:** a worker

assistance *n.* help

hastily *adv.* in a hurry

locomotives *n.* plural of **locomotive:** a train engine

thrive *v.* to succeed; to grow well

Practice Write the vocabulary word that best matches the underlined word or phrase in the sentences below.

1. Would you like some <u>help</u> getting that jar off the top shelf? ____assistance____

2. Have you ever traveled on a <u>coast-to-coast</u> railroad? ____transcontinental____

3. July <u>quickly</u> finished her chores so she could go to the circus.
   ____hastily____

4. Miriam and Derrick both painted their toy <u>train engines</u> green.
   ____locomotives____

5. Watch out for those <u>swarming</u> bees in the backyard. ____buzzing____

6. Our neighbor hired 20 <u>workers</u> to pick apples in his orchard. ____laborers____

Name _____   Date _____

Fact and Opinion

Focus Writers use facts and opinions to support ideas in their writing.

- A **fact** is a statement that can be proven true.
  Chicago is a city in the state of Illinois. (You can prove this statement by finding Chicago on a map of Illinois.)

- An **opinion** is what someone feels or believes is true. An opinion cannot be proven true or false.
  Chicago is the best city in the world. (This statement cannot be proven true or false. It is a statement about what someone believes.)

Practice A **Read the following sentences. Ask yourself the question, "Can this sentence be proven true?"**
If it can be proven true, then it is a fact. Write an *X* next to each sentence that is a fact.

1. __X__ Two plus two equals four.

2. _____ The color red is better than yellow.

3. _____ Eggs should be eaten for breakfast only.

4. __X__ An eagle has feathers and wings.

5. __X__ A library is a place where people borrow books.

6. _____ In-line skates are better than bicycles.

7. __X__ Apples are not oranges.

8. __X__ Pure maple syrup is tapped from the maple tree.

Comprehension Skill • *Reteach*

Name _____   Date _____

Fact and Opinion

Practice B **Read the following sentences. Ask yourself the question, "Can this sentence be proven true or false?" If it cannot be proven true or false, then it is an opinion. Write an *O* next to each sentence that is an opinion.**

9. _____ Five plus five equals ten.

10. __O__ A shirt with short sleeves is better than one with long sleeves.

11. _____ Mars is the closest planet to Earth.

12. __O__ Socks should always be worn with shoes.

13. _____ Foxes prey on small animals.

14. __O__ Everyone should learn to swim.

Read the paragraph below. The paragraph has both facts and opinions. Draw one line under the facts. Draw two lines under the opinions.

All whales should remain in their natural environment. Whales live in both the Pacific and Atlantic Oceans. They live in groups and communicate with one another. I don't think whales should be captured and separated from their families.

Apply **What's your opinion about whales? Write a sentence stating your opinion.**

Possible Answer I think whales should remain free.

_____

_____

Name _____ Date _____

Greek Roots

Focus Many English words contain **Greek roots.** If you know the spellings and meanings of common Greek roots, you can figure out how to spell and define words that contain the roots.

biome	prototype	chronology	architect	chronicle
monarch	bionic	thermometer	hydrant	hydrogen

Practice **Meaning Strategy**
Choose the correct spelling word to complete the sentence. Use a dictionary as needed.

1. The desert (biome, chronicle) is very dry. _____biome_____

2. The historian will (chronology, chronicle) the events of the last century.
_____chronicle_____

3. He has had a (chronic, typical) cough for weeks. _____chronic_____

4. She used a (thermometer, thermostat) to check my temperature.
_____thermometer_____

5. The (monarch, architect) designed the new building. _____architect_____

6. The (monarch, architect) has been in power for many years. _____monarch_____

7. The firefighter checked the (hydrate, hydrant) periodically. _____hydrant_____

8. The engineers developed a (chronicle, prototype) of the new car.
_____prototype_____

Name _____ Date _____

Prepositions

Focus

Rule	Example
• A **preposition** is a word that relates a noun, pronoun, or group of words to some other word in the sentence. Some prepositions are *in, to, for, over, before,* and *from.*	• Jane Goodall studied chimpanzees **in Africa.**
• A **prepositional phrase** is a group of words that begins with a preposition and ends with a noun or pronoun.	• Michael Jordan led the Chicago Bulls **to six NBA championships.**

Practice Look at the following groups of words. Write an *X* next to each group of words that is a prepositional phrase.

1. __X__ in science class

2. __X__ at her desk

3. _____ went home

4. __X__ during the 1940s

5. _____ the president spoke

6. __X__ at violin practice

7. _____ animals stretched

Apply

8. Write a sentence using the prepositional phrase *at the game.*

Possible Answer My dad and I met Uncle Roger at the game.

Name _____ Date _____

Latin Roots

Focus Many of the English words we use today contain roots that have been borrowed from the Latin language.

Here are some common **Latin roots** and their meanings.

rupt = "break"	**nat** = "born"	**struct** = "build"
cap = "head"	**vis** = "to see"	**sol** = "alone"
flect or **flex** = "bend"	**cred** = "believe"	**form** = "shape"

Practice **Write two words using each of the following Latin roots.**

1. **form**   **Possible Answer** inform, reform

2. **cred**   **Possible Answer** credit, credible

3. **flect**   **Possible Answer** reflect, inflection

4. **sol**   **Possible Answer** solo, solace

5. **vis**   **Possible Answer** vision, visible

6. **cap**   **Possible Answer** cap, captain

7. **struct**   **Possible Answer** destructive, construct

8. **nat**   **Possible Answer** nature, native

9. **rupt**   **Possible Answer** interrupt, rupture

Name _____ Date _____

Selection Vocabulary

Focus

muscular *adj.* having well-developed muscles

generous *adj.* kind and unselfish

strain *v.* to hurt yourself by trying to do too much

bulged *v.* past tense of **bulge:** to swell out

legend *n.* a story passed down through the years that is not entirely true

versions *n.* plural of **version:** a particular telling of a story

Practice **Circle the correct word that completes each sentence.**

1. The bodybuilder's arms are quite _____.
   a. strain   **b.** legend   **c. muscular**

2. I read a _____ of Johnny Appleseed.
   a. legend   **b.** versions   **c.** generous

3. I hope he didn't _____ a ligament in his knee.
   a. bulged   **b.** generous   **c. strain**

4. Our book bags _____ with videos and books from the library.
   a. strain   **b.** muscular   **c. bulged**

5. Many different _____ of George Washington's biography have been written.
   a. legend   **b. versions**   **c.** generous

6. Our teacher encourages us to be _____ with each other.
   a. generous   **b.** muscular   **c.** legend

Name _____ Date _____

Drawing Conclusions

Focus **Drawing conclusions** helps readers get more information from a story. Here is how you draw conclusions.

- Look for bits of information, or details, about a character or an event in a story. Use these details to make a statement or draw a conclusion about that character or event.

- Sometimes the conclusion is already stated in a sentence in the story.

Practice A **Look at the groups of sentences below. The sentences in the first column are details. The sentences in the second column are possible conclusions. One conclusion is correct, and one is incorrect. Put an X next to the sentence that could be the conclusion to the first pair of sentences. The first one is done for you.**

Details	Conclusions
1. Brad likes fruit.	_____ Brad hates apples.
Apples are fruit.	__X__ Brad likes apples.
2. Connor loves animals.	__X__ Connor loves dogs.
Dogs are animals.	_____ Dogs love animals.
3. Samantha likes outdoor sports.	_____ Samantha does not like soccer.
Soccer is an outdoor sport.	__X__ Samantha likes soccer.
4. Ten pennies equal ten cents.	_____ One dime is worth more than ten pennies.
One dime equals ten cents.	__X__ Ten pennies equal one dime.

Comprehension Skill • *Reteach*

Name _____ Date _____

Drawing Conclusions

Practice B   **Read the paragraph. Then answer the following.**

    Mrs. Golding put a soup bone on a dish. Planning to make soup later, she put the dish on the counter in the kitchen. Grover, her dog, was watching her closely. He would take the bone when given a chance. The front doorbell rang. Mrs. Golding left the kitchen to answer the door. When she walked back into the kitchen, both the dog and the bone were gone.

5. The sentences in this paragraph contain many details. One detail tells that Grover watched Mrs. Golding closely. Write two more details you find in this paragraph.

Detail: **Possible Answer** Mrs. Golding placed a soup bone in a dish on the

counter.

Detail: **Possible Answer** The doorbell rang and Mrs. Golding left the room.

6. From the details in this paragraph, what can you conclude?

Possible Answer The dog jumped onto the counter and took the bone.

Apply   **Read the following pair of statements, and draw a conclusion. Write your sentence in the spaces below.**

All goats are animals.
Gordon is a goat.

Conclusion: **Possible Answer** Gordon is an animal.

Name _____ Date _____

Latin Roots

Focus

Many English words contain **Latin roots.** If you know the spellings and meanings of common Latin roots, you can figure out how to spell and define words that contain the roots.

- The Latin root **strain** means "to draw tight."
- The Latin root **legere** means "to read."
- The Latin root **vers** means "turn."
- The Latin root **man** means "hand."

- The Latin root **rupt** means "break."
- The Latin root **sec/seq** means "following."
- The Latin root **prim** means "first or highest."

sequel	**primate**	**legend**	**sequence**	**constraint**
erupt	**abrupt**	**manicure**	**versus**	**adverse**

 **Practice**

Meaning Strategy
Choose the spelling word that correctly completes the sentence.

1. I hope the medicine does not have any ___adverse___ effects.

2. The first movie was so good, I can't wait to see the ___sequel___

3. My aunt goes to the beauty shop for a ___manicure___ every week.

4. We went to the ___primate___ section of the zoo to see the monkeys.

5. I like to read the books in ___sequence___ from first to last.

6. The car came to an ___abrupt___ halt when she slammed on the brakes.

7. The volcano is about to ___erupt___.

8. The ___legend___ on the map showed how far we had to go.

Spelling • *Reteach*

Name _____ Date _____

Prepositional Phrases

> **Focus**
>
> Remember, a **preposition** relates a noun, pronoun, or group of words to another word in the sentence. *(in, through, by, with)*
>
> The noun or pronoun that follows a preposition in a sentence is called the **object of a preposition.** (in the *house,* through the *woods,* by *her,* with *me*)
>
> A **prepositional phrase** *(in the house)* includes a **preposition** *(in)* and its **object.** *(the house)*
>
> Sentences that are related can often be combined by putting some of the information into a prepositional phrase.
>
> Example:
>
> Several women went shopping. My mom brought home the most packages of all.
>
> New, combined sentence:
>
> Of the women who went shopping, my mom brought home the most packages of all.

Practice Combine these pairs of sentences into one sentence using a prepositional phrase.

1. There are many runners in the race. Sarah is in the lead. **Possible Answer** Of all the runners in the race, Sarah is in the lead.

2. I have many jobs to do today. Feeding my dog is the most important job.
   Possible Answer Of all the jobs I have to do today, feeding my dog is most important.

Name _____ Date _____

Synonyms

Focus **Synonyms** are words that have similar meanings.

Examples:

amazing and *incredible*

smart and *intelligent*

Practice

seat anxious	pain journal	automobile thankful	celebration error

Write a synonym for each of the following words from the word box above.

1. grateful _____thankful_____

2. nervous _____anxious_____

3. mistake _____error_____

4. party _____celebration_____

5. diary _____journal_____

6. ache _____pain_____

7. chair _____seat_____

8. car _____automobile_____

Name _____ **Date** _____

Selection Vocabulary

Focus

yearning *v.* form of **yearn:** to long; to wish

dreaded *v.* past tense of **dread:** to fear

translated *v.* past tense of **translate:** to change words or thoughts from one language into another

mainland *n.* the main part of a country, as opposed to an island

wages *n.* plural of **wage:** pay received for work

strikes *n.* plural of **strike:** a work stoppage as a form of protest

Practice   **Match each word on the left to its definition on the right.**

1. strikes
2. mainland
3. yearning
4. wages
5. translated
6. dreaded

a. anticipated with alarm

b. feeling a strong craving

c. money someone is paid

d. refusing to work

e. the primary part of a country

f. to explain something said in another language

Name _____   **Date** _____

Sequence

> **Focus**
>
> **Sequence** is the order in which things happen in a story. A writer uses time-and-order words to help the reader follow the sequence in a story.
>
> Time-and-order words help a reader follow the sequence in a story.
>
> - **Order words** show the order in which things take place. Words such as *first, then, next,* and *finally* show order.
>
> - **Time words** show how time passes in a story. Words such as *spring, tomorrow,* and *morning* show time.

Practice A   **Look at the pictures. Put the pictures in the proper sequence. Write the correct order word under the picture. Use the order words *first, then,* and *finally*.**

finally

first

then

Comprehension Skill • *Reteach*

Name _____   Date _____

Sequence

Practice B **Look at the following sentences about "Immigrant Children." Put the sentences in the proper sequence. Write the correct order word in front of the sentence. Use the order words *first*, *next*, and *finally*.**

1. _____Next_____, immigrants faced an inspector at Ellis Island.

2. _____First_____, immigrants arrived in America hungry, bruised, and hopeful.

3. _____Finally_____, immigrants began their lives as Americans.

Look at the following sentences. Complete each sentence by filling in a time word. Use the time words in the box below.

today	soon	evening
winter	summer	tomorrow

4. Dinner is usually served in the ___evening___.

5. I will wash clothes ___today, tomorrow, or soon___.

6. My grandparents go to Florida in the ___winter___ and stay through March.

**Apply** **Write the last sentence of the following sequence. Use an order word in your sentence.**

First, Gus stood at home base, baseball bat in hand. Next, the pitcher threw the ball, and then Gus swung the bat.

Possible Answer Finally, he hit a home run.

Name _____ Date _____

Synonyms

Focus | **Synonyms** are words that have the same, or nearly the same, meanings.

| wages | limit | salary | boundary | pay |
| edge | income | border | weird | strange |

Practice | **Visualization Strategy**
Circle the correctly spelled word and write it on the blank.

1. wajes, wages _____wages_____

2. paye, pay _____pay_____

3. limitt, limit _____limit_____

4. boundry, boundary _____boundary_____

5. edj, edge _____edge_____

6. bordre, border _____border_____

7. income, inkome _____income_____

8. weird, weard _____weird_____

9. strainge, strange _____strange_____

10. salary, sallary _____salary_____

Name _____ **Date** _____

Sentence Combining with Appositives

An **appositive** is a noun that is placed next to another noun to identify it or add information about it.

Geoffrey, my best friend, was absent from school today.

Friend is an appositive that describes *Geoffrey.*

An **appositive phrase** is a group of words that includes an appositive and words that describe the appositive. *(my best friend)*

An appositive phrase can combine two sentences into one shorter sentence when one of the sentences is additional information about something in the first sentence.

Practice

Change each of the following pairs of sentences into a single sentence, using an appositive or appositive phrase.

1. Tyrone is an avid reader. Tyrone has read forty books since school started.

Possible Answer Tyrone, an avid reader, has read forty books since school

started.

2. My favorite sport is hockey. Hockey starts up again in November.

Possible Answer Hockey, my favorite sport, starts up again in November.

3. Eliot is my dog. Eliot stole food from my plate.

Possible Answer Eliot, my dog, stole food from my plate.

4. Spring is my favorite season. Spring is almost here.

Possible Answer Spring, my favorite season, is almost here.

Name _____ Date _____

Antonyms

Focus **Antonyms** are words that are opposite in meaning.

Examples:

up and *down*

come and *go*

wet and *dry*

Practice **Match each word on the left to its antonym on the right.**

1. asleep
2. plain
3. growing
4. wise
5. trust
6. near
7. simple
8. chilly

a. shrinking
b. distant
c. warm
d. awake
e. fancy
f. disbelief
g. complicated
h. foolish

Name _____ **Date** _____

Selection Vocabulary

Focus

era *n.* a period of history, usually several years long

demand *n.* the desire for a product or service

desperate *adj.* ready to take large risks with little hope of success

borders *n.* plural of **border:** a line where one country or state ends and another begins

ditches *n.* plural of **ditch:** a long, narrow pathway cut in the soil to drain water

locals *n.* plural of **local:** a person who has been living in a place for a long time, unlike newly arrived people

Practice Review the vocabulary words and definitions from "The Dust Bowl." Write two sentences that each use at least one of the vocabulary words.

1. **Possible Answer** My favorite era of history is the early 1800.

   _____

2. **Possible Answer** The locals in my hometown are very loyal to small-business owners.

Name _____   Date _____

Making Inferences

Focus

> **Making inferences** helps a reader understand the total picture in a story.
>
> An **inference** is a statement you make when you read about a character or event in a story.
>
> - Use **information** from the story. Facts and descriptions in a story are types of information you can use to make an inference.
>
> - Combine the information from the story with your **personal experience** or knowledge to make an inference.

Practice A   **Read the paragraph below. Then answer the questions on this page and the next.**

When Brian awoke, he did not remember much about what had happened in the operating room. He remembered the nurse holding a mask over his nose and mouth and telling him to breathe deeply. He remembered feeling very drowsy. Then, everything and everybody in the room disappeared. Now, here he was back in his hospital room. His throat was very sore, but he felt fine. He wondered what actually had happened during the operation.

Brian asked the nurse, "Did Dr. Bryant really take out my tonsils?"

A fact is information you can use to make an inference. In the paragraph above, one fact is that Brian becomes drowsy in the operating room. Write another fact about the paragraph.

Possible Answer He remembered feeling very drowsy.

_____

_____

Name _____ Date _____

What do you know? Maybe you know what a sore throat feels like. Write something else you know that is related to the character or events in the paragraph.

Possible Answer I know a little something about hospital procedures from when I had my tonsils removed.

Practice B Read the following paragraphs. Think about the information and your knowledge about the characters and events in each paragraph. Then, complete each inference below with the correct word.

Madeline's job was to blow up as many balloons as possible. Josh helped hang blue and white streamers in the dining room. Since Dad was the tallest, he hung the big "Happy Birthday" sign over the doorway. Madeline said, "Casey will be very surprised when he comes home!"

Inference: Who is celebrating a birthday? _____ Casey _____

"Don't forget the sunscreen," Mom said. I grabbed the sunscreen from the medicine cabinet and put it in the bag with the rest of the stuff. I said to myself, "Let's see . . . we have three beach towels, an umbrella, and rubber sandals. Oh! I must bring my bucket and shovel. I want to build an enormous sand castle today."

Inference: Where is the family going? _____ to the beach _____

Apply Make another inference from the paragraph above. Write your statement here.

Possible Answer The narrator likes building sand castles.

_____

_____

Name _____ Date _____

Antonyms

Focus **Antonyms** are words that have opposite, or nearly opposite, meanings.

demand	despair	request	hope	strangers
hollow	locals	solid	alert	drowsy

Practice **Proofreading Strategy**
Circle the misspelled words and write them correctly.

1. I hoap we won't be strangirs for long. ___hope,___ ___strangers___

2. The locles are very actave in their community. ___locals,___
___active___

3. I want a solad gold keychain for my birthday. ___solid___

4. He will reqest his favorite song to dance to. ___request___

5. We will alurt you of any changes. ___alert___

6. The holow tree was a home for many animals. ___hollow___

7. It is important to dimand fair treatment for all people. ___demand___

8. The victims of the tornado were filled with dispare when their homes were
destroyed. ___despair___

Spelling • *Reteach*

Name _____   **Date** _____

Keeping Verb Tenses Consistent

Focus **Verb tenses** within a sentence or paragraph should be kept consistent. When different verb tenses are used, the sentence sounds awkward.

Incorrect: The pitcher *dropped* her glove and *pick* up the ball with her bare hands.

Correct: The pitcher *dropped* her glove and *picked* up the ball with her bare hands.

Practice **Circle the correct verb in parentheses.**

1. Meg's mom told her to finish her lunch and (wash/washed) her hands.

2. Lainey (runs/ran) to the mailbox and checked for mail.

3. Missy read the last page and (close/closed) her book.

4. My mom is working late and (brings/bringing) home a pizza.

5. Did you remember to wash your face and (brush/brushes) your teeth?

6. The store was closed when we got there, so we (go/went) to a different one.

7. I (can't/couldn't) remember his name, so I called him "buddy."

8. Bryan brought snacks for everyone, but he (forgets/forgot) the napkins at home.

Name _____ Date _____

Contractions

A **contraction** is a shortened form of two words. It is formed by combining two words and leaving out one or more letters. It includes an apostrophe to show where the letter or letters have been left out.

Examples:

it is = it's

you will = you'll

should not = shouldn't

Practice Circle the correct contraction in parentheses.

1. Parker (couldn't/could've) figure out the answer to the question.

2. (She'd/She's) like to know when you want to leave for the museum.

3. (I'm/I'd) rather tired after our rafting trip.

4. Gayle told me she (doesn't/don't) like guacamole.

5. Nicholas said (he's/he'll) clean the garage tomorrow.

6. I wonder why (they'll/they've) stopped on the side of the road.

7. I (won't/wouldn't) push that red button if I were you.

8. Did your dad say (he'd/he's) pick you up early today?

Name _____ **Date** _____

Selection Vocabulary

Focus

rust *v.* to have the iron parts turn reddish and scaly, then fall away

binoculars *pl. n.* a tool for seeing far away, made of two telescopes joined to allow the viewer to use both eyes

scarlet *adj.* bright red

skim *v.* to move over lightly and swiftly

slip *v.* to put somewhere quickly and secretly

ashamed *adj.* feeling shame; being upset or feeling guilty because you have done something wrong

Practice **Circle the word in parentheses that best fits each sentence.**

1. Deidre thought a metal swing set might (skim/**rust**), so she got a wooden one.

2. The jet skis (**skim**/slip) the surface of the water.

3. I am (scarlet/**ashamed**) to admit that I didn't finish my project.

4. Did you bring the (**binoculars**/scarlet) so we can see the game better?

5. I'll go (**slip**/skim) her gift into my closet.

6. The lorikeet was a beautiful combination of purple, blue, yellow, green, and (**scarlet**/rust).

Name _____ **Date** _____

Homographs

Focus   **Homographs** are words that are spelled the same way, but which have different meanings, and may have different origins and pronunciations.

Example: *pro' ceeds* is a noun that refers to money obtained from a business venture

pro ceeds' is a verb that means "to continue after an interruption."

conduct	content	rebel	refuse	sewer
moped	insert	contrast	reject	sow

Practice

Dictionary Strategy
Read the sentences. Write a sentence using the word in dark print in a different way. Use a dictionary as needed.

Answers will vary

1. The cat is very **content** basking in the sun. _____

2. I will ride my **moped** to your house. _____

3. I **refuse** to tell a lie. _____

4. The **sow** took good care of the piglets. _____

5. Please **insert** your name where it belongs. _____

6. People should **rebel** when laws are unfair. _____

7. He was rewarded for his good **conduct.** _____

8. The **sewer** stitched the buttons on the shirt. _____

9. My sister will **reject** every suggestion I make. _____

10. We were asked to **contrast** the heroes of the two books. _____

Name _____   **Date** _____

Homophones

Focus **Homophones** are words that have the same sound but different meanings and spellings.

The man <u>rode</u> a donkey down the <u>road</u>.

Knowing the meaning of a word is very important when using homophones.

If you do not know the meaning of a homophone, you may use the word incorrectly.

The man <u>road</u> a donkey down the <u>rode</u>. (wrong)

Practice **Use the following homophones to complete the exercise below.**

soul, sole;   flour, flower;   plain, plane;   tale, tail;   weigh, way

Complete each sentence with a homophone from the box.

1. I grazed the ____<u>sole</u>____ of my feet against the wall.

2. A tulip is a spring ____<u>flower</u>____.

3. The passengers boarded the ____<u>plane</u>____ at 7 P.M.

4. The monkey had a short ____<u>tail</u>____.

5. The butcher used a scale to ____<u>weigh</u>____ the meat.

Name _____ Date _____

Selection Vocabulary

Focus

dawn *n.* when the sun comes up

wove *v.* past tense of **weave**: to lace together

pride *n.* a feeling of worth and importance

huddled *v.* past tense of **huddle**: to wrap oneself tightly

pounded *v.* past tense of **pound**: to beat loudly

tremble *v.* shake

embarrassment *n.* a feeling of shyness or being ashamed

dared *v.* past tense of **dare**: to have the courage to do something

Practice **Circle the correct word that completes each sentence.**

1. I spilled my soup and felt _____.
   a. (embarrassment)   **b.** dared   **c.** pounded

2. The boys got out of the cold pool and _____ under their beach towels.
   a. dared   **b.** (huddled)   **c.** pounded

3. Watch the baby horse's legs _____.
   a. dawn   **b.** (tremble)   **c.** wove

4. My mom takes _____ in me even if I don't get first place.
   a. embarrassment   **b.** tremble   **c.** (pride)

5. Jermaine _____ on the drum until his dad asked him to stop.
   a. huddled   **b.** dared   **c.** (pounded)

6. _____ is my favorite time of the day.
   a. Dared   **b.** (Dawn)   **c.** Pride

Homophones

Name _____ **Date** _____

Focus   **Homophones** are words that sound alike. They have different meanings and are spelled in different ways.

• Knowing the meanings of homophones can help us know which spelling to use when words sound alike.

carrot	pride	carat	pried	toad
rays	scent	raise	toed	sent

Practice   **Proofreading Strategy**
Circle the misspelled words. Write the words correctly on the blanks.

1. The horse (pride) the apple from my hand and ate it in one big bite.

   _____pried_____

2. The rabbit ate the (carat) that was fed to him. ____carrot____

3. He took second place in the (toed) jumping contest. ____toad____

4. The visitors (scent) flowers that had a lovely (cent) as a thank you for our

   hospitality. ____sent____   ____scent____

5. The prince gave her a ten (carrot) diamond for her birthday. ____carat____

6. I am trying to (rays) my dog to be polite. ____raise____

7. He gently (toad) the (toed) and made it jump. ____toed____   ____toad____

8. He took great (pried) in his accomplishment. ____pride____

Name _____   Date _____

Sentence Combining with Appositives

Focus

An **appositive** is a noun that is placed next to another noun to identify it or add information about it.

Example: My sister, **Jackie,** starts kindergarten this fall.

Jackie is an appositive that describes *my sister.*

An **appositive phrase** is a group of words that includes an appositive and words that describe the appositive.

Example: Isabel, Lizzie's mother, is waiting for her daughter to come home.

Lizzie's mother is an **appositive phrase** that describes *Isabel.*

- An **appositive** is usually set off by commas next to the noun it identifies.

- **Appositives** are *nouns.*

- Two sentences can be combined into one shorter sentence, using appositives.

Example: I went shopping with my grandma. My grandma is a bargain hunter.

I went shopping with my grandma, the bargain hunter.

**Circle the appositive or appositive phrase in each sentence.
On the line, write the noun that it identifies.**

1. My turtle, (Slowpoke), is the first pet I've ever had. _my turtle_

2. Yamin asked Susan, (the new student), to join our group. _Susan_

3. Mick introduced me to his uncle, (the guitar player). _uncle_

4. Jaysie, (my favorite musician), will be playing in my city tonight. _Jaysie_

5. We're reading my favorite book, (*Charlotte's Web*), in school this month. _book_

Name _____ **Date** _____

Homonyms

Homonyms are words that sound the same and are spelled the same, but have different meanings.

Example: *fan*

A **fan** is a machine that cools.

A **fan** is someone who cheers for a person or team.

Homonyms may be the same part of speech, or they may be completely different parts of speech.

Example: *box*

The competitors **box** in a ring. (verb)

I carefully opened the **box.** (noun)

Practice   Write the word from the box that fits both definitions.

limb	can	kind	will	ram

1. friendly and nice; a type of thing _____kind_____

2. a tree branch; an arm or leg _____limb_____

3. a document stating who inherits your possessions; a strong desire to do something _____will_____

4. a male sheep; to force into place _____ram_____

5. a cylinder-shaped container; the ability to do something _____can_____

Name _____   Date _____

Selection Vocabulary

Focus

clutched *v.* past tense of **clutch:** to hold tightly

longed *v.* past tense of **long:** to want very much

wobbled *v.* past tense of **wobble:** to shake back and forth unsteadily

pruned *v.* past tense of **prune:** to trim tree branches

confident *adj.* sure of oneself

wearily *adv.* in a tired way

perched *v.* past tense of **perch:** to sit on top of something, as a bird does

gleefully *adv.* with great happiness

Practice   **Fill in each blank with a vocabulary word from this lesson to complete each sentence.**

1. I am _____confident_____ that you will enjoy this movie.

2. Caryn wiped her sweaty brow and sat down _____wearily_____.

3. The turtledoves _____perched_____ on the rafters high above us.

4. Quinn grinned and _____gleefully_____ ran off to share the good news.

5. Debra _____longed_____ for the day when her grandparents would return from overseas.

6. The woman nervously _____clutched_____ her purse as she walked through the airport.

7. We _____pruned_____ our pear tree so the fruit would grow better.

8. The cone _____wobbled_____ for a moment and then fell.

Name _____ **Date** _____

Author's Point of View

Focus Every story is told from a specific **point of view** that the author chooses. **Point of view** may be first-person or third-person.

In writing a story, the author creates a narrator who tells the story from a particular point of view.

In a story told from the **first-person point of view,** the narrator is a character in the story. The narrator uses pronouns such as *I, me,* and *my* when telling the story.

In a story from the **third-person point of view,** the narrator is an outside observer looking at the happenings in the story. The narrator uses pronouns such as *he, she,* and *they* when telling the story.

Practice A Look at the sentences below. In the spaces provided, write the point of view of each sentence. Remember, first-person point of view uses pronouns such as *I, me,* and *my.* Third-person point of view uses pronouns such as *he, she*, and *they.*

1. I have three sisters. _____first-person_____

2. They all have brown hair. _____third-person_____

3. She is on the volleyball team. _____third-person_____

4. Caleb told me about his vacation. _____first-person_____

5. He visited Mount Rushmore. _____third-person_____

6. My sister lives in San Diego. _____first-person_____

7. She works for a law firm. _____third-person_____

Name _____ Date _____

Author's Point of View

Practice B Fill in the sentences below, using pronouns that show the first-person point of view. Use the pronouns *I, me,* and *my.*

8. _____I_____ can tell you about the game.

9. Please return _____my_____ CD as soon as you can.

10. Have you met _____my_____ mother?

11. He gave _____me_____ some clues about the mystery.

Fill in the sentences below, using pronouns that show the third-person point of view. Use the pronouns *he, she,* and *they.*

12. _He or She_____ likes playing the piano.

13. _They_____ are driving across the country next summer.

14. _He or She_____ is a college student.

15. _She_____ is Raul's youngest sister.

 **Apply** **Read the passage below. Then answer the questions.**

    Delores loves basketball. She reads books about basketball, she plays basketball wherever and whenever she can, and she is always asking her friend Yolanda to play basketball with her. If Dolores can't play basketball, she imagines winning games. What is the point of view

the passage? _third-person_____

Write the word that tells you the point of view. ___She_____

Name _____ **Date** _____

Homonyms

Focus **Homonyms**/multiple meaning words are words that are spelled and pronounced the same way. They have different meanings and may be different parts of speech.

| batter | squash | figure | pupil | drive |
| general | round | anchor | reflect | glasses |

Practice **Meaning Strategy**
Choose the spelling word that matches the clue.
Then, write a sentence using the word in a different way. Use a dictionary as needed. **Answers will vary.**

1. a student _____pupil_____

2. a vegetable _____squash_____

3. the baseball player that hits the ball _____batter_____

4. help you to see _____glasses_____

5. keeps a boat in place _____anchor_____

6. to move in a car _____drive_____

7. to remember _____reflect_____

8. the shape of a body _____figure_____

9. not detailed _____general_____

10. the shape of a ball _____round_____

Name _____   **Date** _____

Homophones

Focus Remember, **homophones** are words that sound alike but have different meanings.

Example: **They're** going to eat **their** yogurt over **there.**

- **They're** is a contraction for *they are.*
- **Their** is a possessive pronoun and an adjective.
- **There** is an adverb meaning *at or in that place*.

She went **to two** soccer games, **too.**

- **To** can mean *in the direction of,* be used to show an action *to drink,* and show the recipient of an action, as in g*ive it **to** me.*
- **Too** is an adverb meaning *also*, *in addition*, *more than enough*, or *very.*
- **Two** refers to the number *two.*

Look at that cat—**it's** carrying **its** kitten in its mouth!

- **It's** is a contraction for *it is.*
- **Its** is a possessive pronoun, as in *its own family.*

If the underlined word is used correctly in the sentence, write C. If it is used incorrectly, write the correct word on the line.

1. I have <u>too</u> tickets for tonight's game. _____ two _____

2. Did Raymond and Ricky eat all <u>there</u> spaghetti? _____ their _____

3. It looks like <u>its</u> going to rain. _____ it's _____

4. Trent wants <u>two</u> go home soon. _____ to _____

5. <u>They're</u> only in town for one night. _____ C _____

Name _____ **Date** _____

Superlative Adjectives and Adverbs

Focus
- Some adjectives and adverbs are **superlative.** Superlatives often end in -*est.*
- **Superlative adjectives** compare three or more nouns.
- **Superlative adverbs** compare three or more verbs.
- Some superlatives use *most* and do not use an -*est.*

Practice A Look at the following sentences. Decide whether the underlined superlative is an adjective or adverb. Then write *adjective* or *adverb* in the space provided.

1. The Douglas Fir is the <u>tallest</u> tree in our yard. ____adjective____

2. The <u>farthest</u> traveling spacecraft is the Voyager 1 probe. ____adverb____

3. We swim <u>most often</u> during the summer. ____adverb____

4. The Australian sea wasp has the <u>most painful</u> sting of all animals.
   ____adjective____

Practice B

5. Write a sentence using the superlative form of the adjective *cold.*
   Possible Answer Winter is the coldest season.
   _____

6. Write a sentence using the superlative form of the adverb *fast.*
   Possible Answer My sister runs fastest when she wears her favorite
   _____
   sneakers.
   _____

Name _____   **Date** _____

Selection Vocabulary

> **wealth** *n.* a great amount of money
>
> **possessions** *n.* plural of **possession:** a thing that someone owns
>
> **protested** *v.* past tense of **protest:** to say in disagreement
>
> **fine** *adj.* very nice
>
> **demanded** *v.* past tense of **demand:** to ask firmly
>
> **discarded** *adj.* thrown away

Write the word from the word box that matches each definition below.

1. ___discarded___ gotten rid of

2. ___fine___ high quality

3. ___protested___ argued

4. ___demanded___ required

5. ___wealth___ a lot of money

6. ___possessions___ things that belong to someone

Name _____   Date _____

Compare and Contrast

Focus To compare means to tell how things are alike. To contrast means to tell how things are different.

- To **compare** means to tell how two or more things are alike.
  A zebra and a leopard are alike. They are both animals.

- To **contrast** means to tell how two or more things are different.
  A zebra and a leopard are different.
  A zebra has stripes. A leopard has spots.

Practice A Look at the pairs of words. Write how they are alike in the spaces below.

1. string   rope   Both are used to tie things.

2. purse   suitcase   Both are used to carry things.

3. car   motorcycle   Both are used for travel.

4. winter   summer   Both are seasons.

Look at the pairs of words. Write how they are different in the spaces below.

5. string   rope   **Possible Answer** String is thin. Rope is thick.

6. purse   suitcase   **Possible Answer** A purse is small. A suitcase

is large.

Name _____   Date _____

Compare and Contrast

Look at the pairs of things listed below. Write in the spaces how the things are alike and how they are different.

Possible Answers

Things		Alike	Different
elephant	bat	Both are mammals.	An elephant is the largest mammal; a bat is the smallest mammal.
chair	desk	Both are furniture.	You sit on a chair. You sit at a desk.

Think about two things you might compare and contrast. Write the pair of things in the first column of the list below. In the second column, write how these things are alike. In the third column, write how they are different. **Possible Answers**

Things	Alike	Different
pen	They are both used in	You write with a pen.
paper	an office.	You write on paper.

Name _____ Date _____

Comparatives

Focus **Comparatives** are words that end in *-er*. They are adjectives that are used to compare two things.

- Adding *-er* may require changes to the base word.
- Sometimes the *y* at the end of a base word changes to *i* before adding *-er*.

wealthier	fresher	finer	ruder	droopier
firmer	crabbier	luckier	larger	stiffer

Practice **Visualization Strategy**
Add *-er* to the words. Remember you may need to change the base word before adding the ending.

1. wealthy   _____wealthier_____

2. crabby   _____crabbier_____

3. droopy   _____droopier_____

4. fresh   _____fresher_____

5. rude   _____ruder_____

6. stiff   _____stiffer_____

7. large   _____larger_____

8. lucky   _____luckier_____

9. fine   _____finer_____

10. firm   _____firmer_____

Name _____ Date _____

Double Negatives

Focus

In English, we use only one negative word in a sentence. When two negatives occur in a sentence, we say the sentence contains a **double negative.** Some examples of negative words include *no, no one, nobody, none, not, nothing, nowhere,* and *never, aren't, won't, weren't, haven't,* and *isn't.*

Example: We **aren't never** going to finish our homework at this rate.

Corrected sentence: We are **never** going to finish our homework at this rate.

Practice Circle all the negative words in the following sentences. Put an *X* by each sentence that contains a double negative.

1. Zoey (won't) go (nowhere) close to my snake. ___X___

2. February (isn't) (nobody's) favorite month—it's too cold. ___X___

3. Faith (won't) give me (none) of her popcorn. ___X___

4. We (won't) get any painting done if you keep talking. _____

5. You (shouldn't) give her (no) cookies until she eats her vegetables. ___X___

Name _____ Date _____

Contractions

Focus   A **contraction** is a single word made of two words that have been combined by omitting letters. Use an apostrophe in place of the omitted letters.

Examples:

you are = you're

can not = can't

should not = shouldn't

Practice   **Write the contractions formed by the words below.**

1. you have   _____you've_____

2. we will   _____we'll_____

3. that is   _____that's_____

4. he is   _____he's_____

5. do not   _____don't_____

6. will not   _____won't_____

7. they are   _____they're_____

Name _____ Date _____

Selection Vocabulary

daydream *v.* to let the mind wander, to think about things that may not happen

provide *v.* to give something to someone

value *n.* worth or importance

worthless *adj.* of no use or value

miser *n.* a person who loves money more than anything else

misfortune *n.* bad luck

Write the vocabulary word next to the group of words that have a similar meaning.

1. cheapskate; tightwad; scrooge   _____miser_____

2. useless; empty; not valuable   _____worthless_____

3. disaster; mishap; catastrophe   _____misfortune_____

4. imagine; fantasize; envision   _____daydream_____

5. give; supply; bestow   _____provide_____

6. worth; importance; cost   _____value_____

Name _____ Date _____

Superlatives

Focus **Superlatives** are words that end in *-est*.

- They are adjectives that are used to compare more than two things.

- Adding *-est* may require changes to the base word. Sometimes the *y* at the end of a base word changes to *i* before adding *-est*.

strictest	rarest	wildest	fairest	greatest
hungriest	sleepiest	trimmest	hugest	steepest

Practice **Proofreading Strategy**
Write the correctly spelled word on the blank.

1. strictest, stricttest ___strictest___

2. greatest, greattest ___greatest___

3. rarrest, rarest ___rarest___

4. fairrest, fairest ___fairest___

5. hungriest, hungryest ___hungriest___

6. trimest, trimmest ___trimmest___

7. steppest, steepest ___steepest___

8. sleepiest, sleepyest ___sleepiest___

9. huggest, hugest ___hugest___

10. wildest, wilddest ___wildest___

Name _____ **Date** _____

Combining Sentences with Participial Phrases

- A **participle** is a verb form used as an adjective. It usually ends in *-ed* or *-ing*.

- A **phrase** is a group of words that may contain a verb but not the verb's subject.

- A **participial phrase** is a group of words that begins with a participle and modifies a noun or pronoun.

Example: **Sprinting to the car,** Shannon beat her brother by a second.

Participial phrases can be used to combine two sentences, making your writing flow smoother.

Example: Jimmy watched his baby sister chew on his new book. At the same time, he was frowning.

New sentence: Frowning, Jimmy watched his baby sister chew on his new book.

Practice **Read the following sentences. Underline the participial phrase and circle the noun or pronoun it describes.**

1. (Abby), laughing loudly, woke up her father from his nap.

2. Hoping he would enjoy it, (Erin) bought her brother a new football.

3. Meowing softly, my (kitten) rubbed her body up against my leg.

4. Knowing his teacher liked oranges, (Eduardo) brought her one as a gift.

5. Listening to her favorite song, (Reza) danced around the room.

Comparative Adjectives and Adverbs

Focus

- Some adjectives and adverbs are **comparative.** Comparatives often end with -er.
- **Comparative adjectives** compare two nouns.
- **Comparative adverbs** compare two verbs.
- Some comparatives use *more* and do not use an -er ending.

Practice A Look at the following sentences. Decide whether the underlined comparative is an adjective or adverb. Then, write *adjective* or *adverb* in the space provided.

1. Walking up a hill is <u>easier</u> than climbing a mountain. _____adjective_____

2. A blue whale is <u>bigger</u> than a hummingbird. _____adjective_____

3. My uncle sings <u>more loudly</u> than my aunt. _____adverb_____

4. Stacey is <u>older</u> than Mark. _____adjective_____

Practice B

5. Write a sentence using the comparative form of the adjective *short.*

   Possible Answer The step stool is shorter than the ladder.

6. Write a sentence using the comparative form of the adverb *early.*

   Possible Answer My sister wakes up earlier than I do.

Name _____   Date _____

Selection Vocabulary

Focus
> **opposing** *adj.* on the other side of an issue
>
> **investment** *n.* money someone puts into a business in order to make more money
>
> **stencils** *n.* plural of **stencil:** a cut-out pattern used for making letter shapes with paint or markers
>
> **partner** *n.* someone who owns a business with another person
>
> **profits** *n.* plural of **profit:** money a business earns
>
> **century** *n.* a span of one hundred years
>
> **corny** *adj.* old-fashioned or sappy
>
> **product** *n.* item that is sold by a business

Practice Circle the word in parentheses that best fits each sentence.

1. Your jingle is (**corny**/opposing) but it works.

2. What kind of (opposing/**investment**) are you thinking of making in the business?

3. Gianna bought a package of (product/**stencils**) to paint her house number on her mailbox.

4. Ingrid asked Rosa to be her (**partner**/stencils) in a new business.

5. My little brother wasn't even born in the 20th (corny/**century**).

6. Ray decided to focus on selling just one (profits/**product**) in the beginning.

7. The two brothers agree on many things, but they have (**opposing**/partner) political viewpoints.

8. We should definitely save some of our (**profits**/product), and not spend them all right now.

Name _____ **Date** _____

Contractions

Contractions are shortened forms of two words.

- Contractions are made by leaving out at least one letter and using an apostrophe instead.
- Some contractions are homophones, meaning they sound alike but are spelled differently.

wouldn't	let's	you've	they've	you're
who's	hadn't	you'll	I'd	where's
here's				

Practice **Conventions Strategy**
Write a spelling word to replace the boldface words.

1. **Let us** see **who is** at the door. _____Let's,_____ _____who's_____

2. **Here is** the pizza **you have** been waiting for. _____Here's,_____ _____you've_____

3. **Where is** the suitcase **you will** be using for the trip. _____Where's,_____
_____you'll_____

4. I **had not** been home long when she called. _____hadn't_____

5. **They have** decided to move to New York. _____They've_____

6. **You are** a very good friend. _____You're_____

7. I **would not** want to get too close to a grizzly bear. _____wouldn't_____

8. I **would** be happy to go with you. _____I'd_____

Name _____ Date _____

Comparative Adverbs

Focus   **Comparative Adverbs** compare two actions.

To form comparative adverbs, add *-er* to most one-syllable adverbs and use *more* with most adverbs with two or more syllables.

Practice   **Circle the correct adverb form in the parentheses.**

1. Between the two swimmers, Frances swims (faster/more fast)

2. Both dogs dug holes in the backyard, but the bigger dog dug (deeper/more deep)

3. Mary is a beautiful singer, but James sings (more beautifully/beautifuler)

4. David writes (clearer/more clearly) than his little brother.

5. The train will arrive (sooner/more soon) than the bus.